YES, BARBARA, THERE IS AN AIKEN.

Hugs.
Marti Healy

This, and other selected columns, by

MARTI HEALY

originally written for the

Aiken Standard

VOLUME ONE

ISBN 978-0-9857018-2-6

First Edition

Printed in U.S.A.

Photography © by Marti Healy, with the following exceptions:

Photo on page 39 courtesy of Robbie Knox
Photo on page 43 courtesy of and © Shelly Marshall Schmidt
Photo on page 111 courtesy of and © George Edward Buggs
Photos on pages 169 and 172 courtesy of Barry Doss
Photo of author on book cover flap courtesy of Kathy Huff

Published by
The Design Group Press, LLC
www.thedesigngrouppress.com

With great appreciation and affection for the town of
Aiken, South Carolina,
and all its people and animals – my neighbors and friends.

The columns

Foreword

In 2004 I discovered Aiken, South Carolina. I was introduced to it by my closest friend (a long-time horseman) and I decided to move here as soon as possible. I believe it's best to do that sort of thing with a Brigadoon kind of place — quickly, unhesitatingly. And I've never found a place more likely to disappear into the mists of time and imagination than Aiken.

It was the summer before I turned 60. I don't know if that was significant or not. But what did turn out to be significant was that circumstances put me here several years before my friend was able to make the transition, too. It meant I came here knowing no one, having visited just two times. I bought my house over the phone, long distance, after seeing it only once. My moving van got lost and tangled with a hurricane and left me without any of my possessions (those tangible things that somehow seem to define us) for week after week, stranding me with a roof over my head, the clothes on my back, two confused yet willing cats, and very little else. So this was how I came to Aiken. Alone, my heart in my hand, my life wide open.

From the beginning, I was embraced and valued and treated with every kindness by everyone with whom I came into contact. I was invited to things and places and shown the treasures of the town; I touched its history and heard its stories, was intrigued with its culture and wrapped in its hospitality. Because of this uniquely Southern greeting, I began writing columns about my experiences for the local newspaper, the *Aiken Standard*. They asked for six columns initially. Eight years and 146 columns later, I have stopped to take a breath and a loving look back.

This book is a personally selected collection of 50 of those columns.

Recently, a friend described these columns as "short stories." I think I agree. Each is a sort of small vignette, a mini story, about something or someone or someplace I have come to know because I came to Aiken. A place or person or experience that has enriched me and my love for this incredible town.

Many of my stories are about dogs. I came with none, but have acquired and hosted several of them since my move here. Many of the stories are about cats. I arrived with two and still have two, but not the same combination of them. A good many of the stories are also about the people I have met here. Wonderful people both living today and alive in the past. But mostly, these stories are about the place — more specifically, the "sense of place" that I have found in Aiken that is like nowhere else I have ever known.

I was a professional writer for 30 years before I moved here and had already authored one book. But since I've come to Aiken, I have been able to write two novels based on my experiences here, with two more books in various stages of development, and the beginning of a third (with many more still whispering behind my consciousness). Aiken is, indeed, a place deep with inspiration. However, I feel I should state for the record that I do not now, nor will I ever be likely to, claim to be a "Southern writer." This is a very special and rightfully proud breed of person, I have come to understand. I will forever be a "Northerner," looking in from the outside. But I am looking in with the deepest respect and fascination and love for my adopted home: the South in general, and South Carolina in particular, with a town called Aiken at the very heart of it all.

I hope you enjoy these short stories about the place I love and the people in it. I hope you find the love and respect woven into each vignette. It is with great privilege and pleasure that I invite you to share with me this place that may sound "too good to be true," but does, indeed, exist. If you don't believe me ... ask Barbara. Or just read the column on page 64.

The Rhythm of Aiken.

Do you believe a place can have its own distinct rhythm? I do. Just as surely as the pulling of the tides and the pounding of the surf. Just as meaningful as the beating of a heart. And just as mysterious as the throaty purr of a contented cat.

I believe every place has its own unique rhythm. And I believe we are either in or out of sync with it.

This thought became most evident to me when I recently had to be away from Aiken for a number of days. Much too long.

I understand about cadence in writing: Dickens' "It was the best of times, it was the worst of times. . ." is one of the most famous examples. Whether we know it or not, as readers, we are strongly influenced by an author's use of cadence and rhythm. The spoken word is no less impacted.

Dance and poetry, music and even exercise have a decided rhythm at their cores. Even the seasons come and go with a rhythm – sliding in and out on the wind, in sync with the sun and moon.

But these are things that have been created by nature or man. What about a place? What is the rhythm of a place? How is there a rhythm of a place?

I have noticed some things about Aiken that may account for its rhythm. For instance, when people greet each other here, they hug. Not always, of course. But a lot. They hug or shake hands or pat an arm or pet the dog. This leads to smiles and "how are yous." There's no rushing into the topic at hand. No business first. Warmth and hospitality are a part of Aiken's rhythm.

People up north say "hi." People in Aiken say "hey." It's slower and sweeter and carries a touch of good humor with it. That "hey" is a part of Aiken's rhythm.

People in Aiken go to church. And places of business don't open until after. This is not to say that people here have more faith than in other places. Or that they live a faithful life any more consistently. And not all people in Aiken do attend a place of worship. But most do. And all can. And hearing church bells, and sitting quietly and listening, and pausing to think of something larger than oneself is a powerful way to feel a spiritual rhythm; and this, too, is a part of Aiken's overall rhythm.

In Aiken, manners matter. People say "please" and "thank you," "Ma'am" and "Sir." They hold the door and hold their tongue. They wait for their turn, and then give it to someone else. They say nice things to each other and hold hands. And it's hard to rush along in your own little self-absorbed world when you're holding someone else's hand. This is a part of Aiken's rhythm.

There are so many other ways about Aiken that contribute to its rhythm and pace and cadence. There are horses' hooves and multi-course meals, art shows and music recitals, soft summer nights with crescent moons, and raindrops that slide over scented trees.

Most of us who live here in Aiken understand it. We're in sync with it. And when I flew back home after being gone too many days, I drove first not to my own house, but to the heart of downtown Aiken. I walked around and watched and listened and felt the sun on my back. I wrapped myself again in the warmth and the rhythm of Aiken.

Admittedly, I am only a newcomer. I have been here less than a year. But I have felt in step with Aiken since the very beginning. Now, its rhythm is my own. Now, away from this place, I am out of step, out of pace.

I believe in the rhythm of Aiken. It has become like the rhythm of my heart.

(February 2, 2005)

Coming home.

I remember hearing or reading somewhere that you should always live in a house that's older than you are. I don't know the reasoning behind the statement, but I rather like the idea.

My house here in Aiken doesn't quite fit the requirement. But we're within the same general decade of each other. And we have close to the same amount of nicks and flaws and uneven places. For both of us, I like to believe it adds "character" and interest. It's a part of the patina that comes only with knowing a bit of life.

When I first fell in love with Aiken and knew I would be living here, I determined I would live as close in to town as I could afford.

One of the things that had attracted me to Aiken in the first place were the amazing houses in and around downtown. From stunning mansions to delightful cottages. Gorgeous estates and quaint and rambling affairs. What impressed me most was how Aiken revered its old homes.

So many communities today too readily tear down old houses and replace them with newly constructed way-too-much structures that lack all the charm and history and character of the originals.

But here in Aiken, people celebrate the past. They may add to a house extensively, even to the point of absorbing it completely in some cases. But even then, it's done with caring and grace and respect. And perhaps a touch of eccentricity.

Obviously, I'm not alone in my appreciation of old Aiken homes and history. The Historic Aiken Foundation was formed more than 30 years ago to help insure the protection and preservation of houses, buildings and neighborhoods. And today, I have found almost everyone in Aiken honors and treasures its past and the structures that so poignantly and beautifully represent it.

The search for my house ended on Brandy Road. I particularly enjoyed the light-heartedness reflected in the street names in the area: Whiskey, Brandy, Gin, Sherry. I understand our current wonderful Mayor Cavanaugh once lived just down the street. Even more "history."

Mine was a Savannah River Site house. A well-proportioned, sturdy brick, with hardwood floors and lots of windows. Well thought out. Thoughtfully built.

But what attracted me most were its bits of nonsense. Doors that opened the wrong way; cupboards that were not symmetrical. The unexplained window in the laundry room door. The doors that were out of alignment or missing altogether. A light switch that was half hidden behind a cupboard. And one that is so high up I have to stand on a chair to reach it.

Interestingly, the fireplace chimney tilts somewhat. And most of the floors sag and squeak reassuringly. But it's a solid, well-loved home that made me smile immediately.

And I have also experienced a great sense of not exactly "déjà vu" here – but a certain "knowing." I just knew the TV room should have two glass-paneled doors at either end; and out behind the guest cottage were leaning two old glass-paneled doors. I have dragged a large double roll of wallpaper with me across the country that I bought more than 20 years ago and had no where to use; but it's perfect for my bathroom here. Stained glass panels that collected dust in my last attic fit in a double window here as if they were custom-made.

I knew exactly where to put the piano and my bed and the cats' dishes. And it was "mine" from the day I moved in.

I have felt the specialness of Aiken even before I moved here. This old house was empty then. I can believe it was waiting just for me to find it, and smile, and come home.

(February 16, 2005)

Saving the best for last.

To the regular readers of my column, I would like to apologize. My last column, appearing in the February 16th edition ("Coming Home."), ended rather abruptly. This is because the last paragraph inadvertently got dropped when it went to press.

Not that my words are so valuable, or that my thoughts are very special, but the last paragraph was what tied everything together, where I made my ultimate point. This is typically the way I structure my columns. Everything leads up to a final point – a reason for being. A conclusion.

So when this particular column appeared without the last concluding paragraph, it made me consider: Perhaps there is a lesson to be learned here. Perhaps I shouldn't save the best bits for last – in my column or in life.

I remember as a child, my mother always set a meal completely on the table at one time. And I always preferred to eat my dessert first. I believe my mother's theory was that as long as we ate everything, it didn't much matter in which order. I also remember getting new clothes and shoes for school and wearing them immediately. None of this saving it for a special occasion. I even remember being allowed to play a tune or two on the piano *before* I practiced my scales. So, apparently, I haven't always saved the best for last. Over the years, however, it must have developed as a habit. And I suspect I'm not alone in this approach to life. (Eat up all the old cookies before you open a new box. Study for the class you hate before the one you love.) But now, I am reconsidering. Now, I think it is a rather sad way to do things – using one's life up saving the best for last.

Ever since I moved to Aiken, I have delighted in the way Aiken never saves its best for last. It is constantly giving us wonderful things to do and enjoy every day. And people instinctively know it. Friends say "let's go" and we go. Someone says "look at this" and we stop to appreciate. There are sunsets and Carolina moons and soft Southern accents that make it warm and welcoming and lovely to be right here, right now.

One friend recently took me for a spontaneous Sunday afternoon ride through Hitchcock Woods on a small horse-drawn carriage, with a second horse and a dog along for good measure. It was cool and damp and wonderfully Aiken. There were thick trees and thrilling hills and deep peace and a natural reverence. We passed walkers and riders and someone practicing jumps. And on the way back, there was a croquet player to chat with – waiting hopefully for others to seize the moment and join in the game. There were people in stables and some out for drives with puppies on their laps. And more dogs and walkers and folks to wave at who always waved back.

Another friend joined me the other night for a last-minute show at the planetarium on the campus of USCA. It began with a trip back in time and imagination, and ended with a magnified peek at the actual moon – all magnificent craters and incredibly mysterious and ageless and awesome.

And just a few weeks ago, two road puppies crossed my path. I picked them up on instinct and impulse. I was waiting to get another dog – someday. "Saving" it for later, I guess. But here we are, right now, two puppies. And no one lives life more in the present than delightfully innocent, everything-is-new, happy-to-be-us pups. A fabulous life-lesson on four legs.

So please forgive my abruptly ending column last time. And for perhaps saving "the best bit" for last. Aiken is overflowing with opportunities to live the best there is right now. And I, for one, am determined to appreciate it to its fullest.

I am also quite positive that I will never leave this exceptional place. I have lived in numerous parts of the country and traveled beyond its borders. And Aiken is where I choose to be – right now, and for the rest of my life. So perhaps, once again, I have saved the best for last. *(March 2, 2005)*

IN MEMORY OF MAGGIE.

Five weeks and three days ago, two little "road puppies" came into my life. Today, one of them left it. Maggie died this morning. A piece of my heart went with her. I didn't expect to love something so small so much in such a short time.

Maggie was just three months old. She had a funny little monkey face – no single breed quite evident. She used to snuggle close against my chest with her tiny head tucked under my chin, all quiet and still and warm. But she could also take a flying leap and pin her larger, rowdier sister pup to the ground with pure glee.

She adored cats, Sparkey in particular. Whenever he came into view, Maggie's tail wagged her entire behind and she wiggled with joy to lick his ears and whiskers. He graciously complied, tolerating her infant enthusiasm with considerable grace. Perhaps he knew.

I think Sophie knew, toward the end. Sophie was her littermate. But no one would have suspected that they shared any parentage by looking at them. This last week, Sophie would rush to Maggie's "sick room" as soon as she came in from outside – just to check on her, often bringing her a prize. Sometimes a stick, or a favorite toy, once a flower. She'd carefully drop the offering over the baby gate at the doorway.

Maggie was never very strong. Her fragility passed first into obvious illness and then rapid decline. But for the few weeks in which I knew her, she was my hero. She was gentle and generous, patient and utterly courageous, and grateful for every kindness. She had silky hair and soft puppy breath. Her ears flopped. Her eyes were wise. I will remember Maggie's eyes.

Maggie left my life as quickly as she entered it. And I am better for having loved her. But right now, I am feeling the loss rather keenly. And I trust you will understand if this column is briefer than usual.

First, however, I want to acknowledge the exceptional compassion shown to me by my neighbors Sandy and Patsy who loved her too and cried with me. And "Dr. Trey" of Palmetto Vet Calls whose skill is considerable and whose heart is great. Thank you my friends.

And to big puppy sister Sophie: I'll walk the rooms of the house with you and the yard out back as you search for her until you realize, without understanding, that "Mags" is gone. And I'll try to help you grieve.

Five weeks and three days ago, God blessed me with two precious creatures to love. This morning, He called Maggie home.

(March 16, 2005)

PRESERVING OUR FAMILY HISTORY.

For the past few days, I have been framing and hanging old family photographs. I am fortunate that my ancestors on both sides of the family seemed to have embraced the invention of the camera and were prolific in their use of and experimentation with it.

On my mother's side, these amateur artists apparently even developed their own photos and explored the possibilities of color printing – often with rather creative results (noting especially the pink cows and all-blue landscapes).

My father's family concentrated more on composition. One photo in particular intrigues me. The shot is taken from outside of an old and weathered house, closely focused on a set of double windows. The windows are open, and intricate lace curtains hang waiting for a summer breeze. The image is brown and faded, but still visible in the lower edge of one of the windows, peeking above the sill, is a small child's head – its soft hair and curious eyes barely visible in the shadows.

Another such captured moment shows a toddler sitting outside on a well-worn wooden porch. He's dressed carefully for warmth – although the shadows indicate a bright sun. Perhaps it is an early Spring morning or a crisp Autumn afternoon. In one small hand, he clutches a home-baked cookie. In the other, a not very willing kitten. (Soft cats and warm cookies – life doesn't get much better than that.) But, to my eye, what makes this photo special is the dog sitting on the far right and so close in the foreground that it is slightly out of focus. While the child is blissfully unaware of the camera, the dog is looking straight into the lens – a little suspicious and obviously protective of her unwary charge.

What draws me to these and other such photographs (culled from a large black trunk full of them) are their inherent "stories." My family story. This is my family history captured and preserved. They invite my mind to put the moments into context. And they compel me to pass this legacy on to following generations.

Fortunately, I know that the child on the porch with the cookie, the cat and the dog is my father. I even know the dog's name. Because Dad has verbally passed this information on to me. Unfortunately, I don't know who the child in the window was. The only story behind that image is in my imagination. No actual memory was written down or spoken to tell its reality.

Even before this old trunk of photographs was brought to Aiken, I had discovered that this special town is as determined to preserve and share its heritage as I am about my own family's. What delights me most is how everyone here – from shop owners to neighbors to people sitting next to you in a restaurant – are remarkably well-versed in the history of Aiken.

I have thoroughly enjoyed walking tours to hear about the "ghosts of Aiken," and talking to authors about the "horses of Aiken." I love reading about and listening at dinner parties to the history of Aiken through its houses and other architecture. I have thrilled to see horses in Hitchcock Woods continuing a century-old tradition. I have been honored to ride in a carriage parade portraying a past of grace and style. And seeing old photographs and relics from days-gone-by on display and still in use throughout town enriches the stories that are now becoming my own.

I suspect the history of Aiken is so well known partly because it is a living history. It is an ongoing story – an unbroken lineage from past to present. It is a continuing story filled with warmth and personality; with fond memories and a unique culture;

with charm and graciousness and pride and eccentricity. It is a loving portrait of horses and homes, of people and places, and also of its own lace curtains and faces of children and dogs on porches on sunny days.

And, thanks to the pride of place that is deep within the hearts of the people of Aiken, this legacy is passed lovingly from generation to generation. It is treasured and preserved and carefully "framed" for us all.

(March 13, 2005)

LAUGHING WITH SOPHIE.

Today I learned to laugh in dog language.

According to recent studies, science has now proven something that we dog-lovers have known all along: Dogs laugh.

But what I also learned, from an article about the study that my sister sent to me, was how to approximate the sound myself. Start to make the sound of "hee, hee, hee" but without the "ee, ee, ee," it explained. It sounds a bit like a series of quick, tight exhales.

I sat down in the middle of the floor near Sophie, my fairly new, young, remaining road puppy. I started making the sound the best I could. And apparently I got it right. Sophie's head shot up, she looked at me with cocked ears, and ran over to me. And, for a few delightful moments, we had a pretty good laugh together – like a couple of dear friends sharing a private joke.

I need to tell you that, since Maggie's death (Maggie was the other road puppy I had found together with Sophie), Sophie and I have struggled to communicate. Perhaps it is her inherent breeds – which are many and varied. Perhaps it is her extreme puppy-ness – she's not yet six months old. Perhaps it is still our dual grief and a bit of reciprocal resentment over the loss of her sister. I also suspect it is a great deal of my own forgotten patience with youthful independence. But the wedge is unmistakably there. The lack of bonding is a large and lonely gap between us.

So when we shared this wonderful laugh together – when I learned to communicate in her language, in partial repayment for all the "sit/stay/wait/don't-chew-the-cat/no" words she is expected to learn in mine – this was a rather significant step across a bridge that could hopefully bring us together.

It is also important to understand that a dog laugh isn't culturally quite the same as a human one. We people laugh in response to something; whereas, dogs laugh to start something fun.

It's a call to relax – an invitation to play. What a delightful lesson. What a valuable skill. And it reminds me of just one more magical gift I have been given here in Aiken: An invitation to play.

Several weeks ago, when we were having some very hearty winds, I drove past Odell Weeks Recreation Area. Out on an open grassy area, there were two individuals taking full advantage of something the rest of us were simply enduring or trying to avoid. Soaring high above them was a kite. Brilliant colors. Long-forgotten memories. All fluttering and twisting and dipping and skittering high and free. Pure play.

Upon a closer look, I realized these individuals were two mature adults. Not a child in sight. Of course. Why not. It's Aiken. People here know how to play. And they remember to do it. They call each other to do it.

Like the dog laugh that is an invitation to play, Aiken is ever alert to the possibilities. It is full of such invitations. And age is simply a non-issue.

This coming weekend, I am beginning a new decade of life. I am turning 60 years old. For the first time, it is simply a number to me. I shrank a bit at becoming 50; but that turned out to be my very best decade ever. I can't wait to discover what this one will bring.

I also can't help but believe that living in Aiken has been a major contributor to this age indifference I am experiencing. This wonderful place that provides winds for kites and dogs for laughter and open invitations to play.

Time doesn't slip by unnoticed here. Each day is precious and lived. So age seems to lack all relevance. And birthdays are just one more excellent reason to eat ice cream with people you like – and perhaps to share a good laugh with a dog named Sophie.

(April 27, 2005)

THE FAIRIES OF THE CAROLINA BAY.

There are Fairies living in Aiken's Carolina Bay. Sophie and I have seen them. Well, almost. They manage to slip out of sight as quickly as we look. But we are both quite convinced they are there. And I don't believe dogs can be fooled about this sort of thing.

On Earth Day a few weeks ago, my young pup Sophie and I were among those who gathered at the remarkable ecological phenomenon on Aiken's southside (just north of Odell Weeks Recreational Park) to get a tour of this Carolina Bay. It is without a doubt a truly magical place.

Of course, simply having an "enchanted" atmosphere about a place doesn't guarantee the presence of Fairies. But each time Sophie and I return there to walk the quiet, pinestraw paths, we witness more evidence that supports our belief. We uncover more signs. We sense their nearness.

Fairies, as a whole, are an elusive group (to say nothing of the cultural differences between them and humans that make detection and communication a bit tricky).

Some say Fairies are fallen angels from ages ago. Others attribute their existence to evolution — a former conquered society, skilled at building and magic, who were forced into hiding underground after the Celts invaded their country. Still another belief holds that Fairies are spirits caught between Heaven and Hell ... too naughty for one, but too good for the other. I rather think Fairies are a mixture of a number of different backgrounds. At least according to my own personal understanding of them. If one can ever truly understand Fairies.

They're also a complicated lot. They tease. They play tricks. They can mesmerize and cast spells. Some never tell the truth. But they will comfort lost children and guide wandering strangers and return misplaced pocket watches and pens and other personal things. And to some, you must never, ever say "thank you." A complicated lot, indeed.

So what is our evidence that Fairies do exist in this Carolina Bay? Whenever you walk in its surrounding forest, notice how you find yourself always circling the water – the central pond area. Clockwise, counterclockwise, it doesn't seem to matter. But you circle and circle and circle. Never walking a straight or crisscross path.

You'll also notice a number of large, deeply rooted trees upturned, when all the trees around them are standing strong. They have somehow fallen sideways exposing naturally veiled access to the underground. Entrances to Fairies' quarters perhaps? Sophie believes the scent tells the story. She examines each one closely but respectfully – then leaves it abruptly, as if compelled to go. There are also pinecones scattered on the forest floor. But upon closer look, are they scattered? Or are they arranged in an intricate pattern of twos and threes and fours to communicate? Perhaps aligned to point the way to an important gathering?

There is a bridge that Sophie refuses to cross. Low, wooden, a perfect place for Fairies to congregate or dart out of view when they hear human footfalls.

Whenever you're within the area, birds seem to follow you. Watching you. As if Fairies are riding on their backs, close to their wings, hidden among their feathers, urging them on to see what you're up to.

There are heady fragrances and sudden breezes and a silence that compels you to speak only in whispers. And once I found a butterfly wing. A velvety, lacy black and gold pattern. But there was no butterfly attached. Was the source of this wing a different species? Fairies can sometimes be a rowdy bunch, when the full moon glows and the whippoorwills call. And losing a wing might be a most ordinary happening.

Of course, I know the many scientific explanations put forth for the origin of the Carolina Bays. Everything from meteor hits to dinosaur footprints have been speculated. (My personal favorite is the theory involving thousands of fish all beating their fins in unison over an artesian spring. Right. One-two-three, everybody flap.)

But none of these theories explains how water devoid of certain fish or amphibians is somehow spontaneously repopulated. Or how some types of plant life are found there, yet no where else. And why the shapes of all Carolina Bays are similar – elliptical, and all pointing in the same general compass direction – similar to Fairy circles found throughout the ages. Just the way Fairies would naturally design them – a race strong in building skills and magic.

Yes, there are Fairies in the Aiken Carolina Bay. They created it. They're still there to guard and protect it. And who would doubt this in a place as magical as Aiken?

(May 25, 2005)

Fingerprints on a Wall.

On the far right-hand corner of my desk sits a small, round, glass paperweight. Occasionally, it fulfills its purpose of holding down wayward papers. But most of the time it sits alone. A silent memento. Often forgotten, I'm afraid. Yet it has a singular history.

It's one of those clear glass domes that magnifies an item placed under it; a patch of black felt glued to the bottom keeps the item enclosed. I found it – empty – in the cheap section of an antiques store. But it suited my purpose perfectly. Because I tucked within it a small piece of the Berlin Wall – a relic brought to me by family friends. They had picked it up off the ground at the actual site where the wall had stood, shortly after it had been torn down.

In appearance, this piece of the wall is a jagged chunk of light beige cement mixed with chipped brown stones; a few inches long overall, perhaps an inch in width. But whenever I look at it, I see fingerprints. From the hands that built it. The hands that tried to escape over it. The hands that tore it down.

In my mind, the hands that built this wall were hesitant. They loved their country, their beautiful city; yet now they were being forced to divide it – splitting families, putting up boundaries around lives and thoughts, closing in futures, shutting out freedom. They were human hands. They must have hesitated.

In my mind, the hands that tried to escape over this wall were trembling. They were the hands of men, women, even children. They were the hands of people who would leave everything, risk punishment, imprisonment and death for an ideal. Though they trembled, these hands must also have been exceedingly courageous.

In my mind, the hands that tore this wall down were strong and sure and came from both sides. Young and old. Brave and frightened. Acting out of intellect and instinct. These hands belonged to people who had to be very proud of one another.

So this piece of the Berlin Wall itself isn't really important. It's the "fingerprints" on it that matter. The unnamed lives it represents. The human hearts and hands imprinted on it.

And as I look at this small fragment of history, it now makes me think of another wall – one on the far east-side of the town of Aiken. The wall is in the Aiken County Veterans Memorial Park.

I recently spent time in this park, sitting by the fountain, walking gently over the commemorative bricks underfoot, reading the oh-too-many names etched on the black granite wall of all the lives from Aiken County given also in defense of an ideal.

At the top of the wall are the words: "In honor of all veterans – past, present, future." The names engraved are those who have been killed in action. The first name is from World War I – Walter Bell. The most recent is the name of Jason Lyle Moski, who gave his life fighting in Operation Iraq Freedom, and it is achingly fresh, the gold etching still bright within the hollow letters.

What wrenches my heart the most, however, is the amount of blank surface on this wall awaiting names. As if we are somehow compelled to fill it, to fulfill the prophecy of that title at the top " … past, present, future."

It was raining when I visited this place. A slow, quiet drizzle of tear-like drops slid down the surface of the wall, softly curving along the letters of each name. But, in my mind, I saw "fingerprints" again. Fingerprints from the hands of those left behind – those who loved these souls whose names are etched here. Fingerprints from touching the memory of someone special one more time.

I left my fingerprints there, too. In silent thanks, I respectfully reached out and touched Jason's name. And Walter's. Names that must never be forgotten. And then, I touched the blank spaces on the wall. And I prayed with all my heart that this part of the wall would someday be torn down – unused, unneeded.

I prayed that one day, scraps of this un-etched portion of the wall would be relics captured under a glass-domed paperweight on the far corner of someone else's desk. I prayed that only fingerprints would be there.

(June 9, 2005)

PAST PRESENT
FROM MARCH 10, 1871 TO
VIETNAM WAR
1964 – 1975
DWANE ADAMS
JOSEPH ADAMS
JERE BARTON
WAYNE BOYD
BUTLER
USA
USN
USN
USA
USA
USA

GOODNIGHT, SOPHIE.

Sophie, my eight-month-old puppy, loves the water. I suspect that one of the many breeds in her vast genetic makeup may have been a fish. She has a child's wading pool that a neighbor friend gave her after discovering Sophie's obvious delight with all things wet and wonderful, and she spends hours reveling in it.

Sophie is a "free range" dog. She has a doggy door, which allows her unlimited access to a large fenced backyard, along with her pool. At least half a dozen times a day – more as the temperatures rise – she plays in that pool: splashing, jumping, bouncing, rolling, throwing toys in and out. But mostly, she enjoys just lying down and lounging in it, with eyes half shut, her chin resting peacefully on one side and tail draped languidly over the other. Absolute contentment.

For myself, I am a firm believer in natural air and fans. In particular, I love to sleep with all the windows open and listen to the soft, gentle, soothing night sounds that surround us in this beautiful, peaceful, Southern community.

Several nights ago – when it was particularly warm and balmy – I was in bed just drifting off, listening with half an ear to the delicate tones of a distant wind chime, and I remember hearing a small splash in Sophie's pool. I envisioned her stretched out in the cool, quiet water under the moon, and thought what a smart young dog she was. How refreshing that would be after a long, busy day of doing important dog stuff.

I started to slide deeper into sleep with a smile. But somewhere on the edge of consciousness, I heard the plastic slap of her dog door closing behind her. Then, slip-slop, slip-slop, soft doggy feet padding down the hall toward the bedroom. Still blissfully clinging to that lovely trance between sleep and wakefulness, I felt Sophie join me in her spot on the bed. A little "sloosh" sound as she lay down.

When the alarming sensation of cold water on my skin struck simultaneously with the distinct and pungent odor of wet dog fur, I was quite suddenly, quite thoroughly awake.

My feet must have hit the floor in the same instant that my hands pulled the bedding away from the mattress. I remember both cats were airborne. And Sophie's face reflected complete surprise. But amidst the scramble and confusion, there was a good deal of laughter, too. There's never a dull moment with Sophie.

This must have seemed like such a good idea to her. First, you stretch out all peaceful in your pool under the stars. Breathe in the succulent floral scents released into the night air. Watch the moon shadows dance on the water. Then, you come in to share all this pleasantry with your best friends … your family … your pack.

Such a grand idea. Such a right idea. And, regardless of disrupted sleep and disheveled cats, I had to agree.

Yes, Sophie, you are right. With the infinite wisdom of youth and dogs, you are right.

Let's put the bedding into the dryer and both go sit in your pool together. Let's gaze at the beauty of a Carolina crescent moon – a waxing moon that symbolizes growing and becoming, just as I am growing and becoming ever so deeply and lovingly a part of this wonderful hometown of Aiken. We'll soak up the essence of pine trees and gardenias and jasmine and honeysuckle and all the other unique and delightfully Southern aromas. We'll listen for night creatures that coo and trill and squeak and click and sing just for us. We'll try to count the stars.

And then we'll sleep – with heartfelt gratitude for all these blessings that we've come to know in this amazing place: nature's beauty, God's bounty, and one soaking wet puppy. Amen.

(June 22, 2005)

THE KINDNESS OF STRANGERS.

It was a drenching rain. With a great crack of thunder and lightning that flashed the air white, I saw the frail, thin dog creep slowly around the corner of the building. He was soaked through, but didn't seem to notice. He didn't seem to notice much of anything. He was the most dejected, dismal creature I think I have ever seen.

Instinctively, I dashed out, grabbed him, and led him back to my car. He barely reacted to me, but climbed in readily, and lay on the floor exhausted. When I got home, I pulled under the carport, closed the gate, and opened the car door. He chose to stay in the dry safety of his small space. I left him alone, to get comfortable with his new surroundings, but Sophie (my mixed-breed puppy) and I watched him from a nearby window.

He is a lost-and-found four-year-old German Shepherd mix. He told me he'd like to be called "Teddy." He has slept on my sofa for hours on end, and is now eating cautiously. And Sophie is determined to teach him how to play.

Just days after Teddy wandered into my life, I was traveling on business. The trip home became an Odyssey of misery. Bad weather, cancelled flights, no hotel space, closed rental car offices, all combined to strand me in a strange town, without luggage, with no cell phone, in the middle of the night, and no way home. After hours and hours of standing and waiting, running and running, bumpy flights and bumped seating, even this last distant airport was now closing, and I was forced to leave its relative safety.

I walked to the curb, sat on its edge, and couldn't hold back the tears any longer. With my head on my knees, I heard a voice behind me saying: "See that lady over there by the white van? Maybe she can help you." A security guard made the suggestion, then turned and walked away.

The woman transport service van driver heard my story, immediately put me in the back seat of her car, and contacted her boss – who began calling hotels all over town, trying to find a vacancy. Another woman – a fellow passenger – patted me on the arm and said: "If we can't get you into a hotel, you can come home with me and spend the night in my guest room." More exhausted tears told her how much I appreciated her gracious and comforting gesture.

Finally, a room was located. The manager got out of bed to make it up for me and get me checked in. It was 3:00 a.m. And I was being cared for – warmly, thoughtfully, compassionately – by people I didn't know and would probably never see again.

A few hours later, the van driver returned to take me back to the now-open car rental counters. She then waited to personally show me the way to the highway heading home.

Friends and neighbors had pitched in to care for my animals – including Teddy – until I could get back. Another brought me food the minute I returned. Sophie danced and swam for me. Sparkey cat snuggled me. Katie cat looked up and yawned.

Teddy was silent. But he followed me throughout the house – watching me with warm brown eyes full of gratitude and hope. We wrapped around each other on the sofa and slept some more.

Both of us were now safe and warm and dry – thanks only to the charity and kindness of strangers.

And now, both of us were home.

(July 20, 2005)

A DOG WITH LAUGHING EYES.

This is Teddy's story.

I have been asked by many regular readers to tell you more about Teddy, the stray German shepherd mix I found a month ago wandering dazed in a thunder storm. A few columns back, I related the story of finding him. But for awhile, I was afraid I might have no more to tell.

When I brought Teddy home that stormy afternoon, he was barely aware of his surroundings. He wouldn't eat or look at me or even get out of the car on his own.

A thorough check by a vet showed he was about four years old, without any irreversible illnesses or injuries, with the exception of one tragic scar down his cheek. And he had been terribly neglected. He got his shots, without even acknowledging the handling or examination. He was just "there" physically, but not mentally or emotionally.

With Sophie's help (my 9-month-old mixed-breed foundling girl dog), we eventually coaxed Teddy gently into the house. He seemed to at least recognize the presence of Sophie. And Sophie has never met a stranger – of any species.

I had to feed him by hand, bites of moist dog food mixed with white rice. But he didn't eat much. And he wouldn't look at me in the eyes – which I realize is good manners in canine culture, but also showed his lack of human companionship, probably throughout his entire life.

The few times I did look into Teddy's eyes, they were alarmingly vacant – flat and lifeless. They are a beautiful almond shape, almost black in color. But there was no depth to them, no life, no reflection. They were woefully, deeply, sad eyes. It almost broke my heart.

Mostly, Teddy slept. He must have been exhausted. Although I had to leave him for a few days on a business trip, my wonderful friends took very good care of him and reported the same thing. Listless eating, not much interest in anything else, sleeping practically all of the time.

When I got home, however, I did notice a slight change in Teddy's eyes. They were every bit as sad, but not quite so vacant. Every day, for hours on end, Sophie would work at getting him to play. She would bring toys to him. Offer him sticks. Jump and tumble in front of him. Splash him from inside her pool. Nip him on the cheeks and jowls. And Teddy would stand stock still, not responding, not knowing how to respond.

He began following me throughout the house, then. Searching my face. Pleading with me to not abandon him or make him leave. I tried to reassure him that he would never have to go anywhere he didn't want to go. And that he was safe here forever with Sophie and me and the cats, as long as he wanted to stay. But he remained afraid.

Then, Teddy fell ill. The doctor could find no reason. But he would not eat at all. He seemed to be in pain. But there was no real physical cause. Finally, we had to leave it to God and Teddy. Teddy had to want to live.

My best friend was visiting – a virtual "dog whisperer" – and he spent long periods of time talking to Teddy, as did I. The cats would sympathetically rub against him from time to time. Sophie diplomatically just let him be.

On the third day, Teddy made his decision. He began eating. He got a bit of spring into his step. He awkwardly tried to play with Sophie – to which she responded with renewed dedication and silliness.

And his eyes began to glow from within.

Over the past several weeks now, he has gained some weight and we're working on getting his coat into shape. He is playing more fully – even initiating it at times. He is extremely affectionate to me and Sophie and the cats. Still shy with strangers. Still hiding from thunderstorms.

But just a few days ago, I looked at him across the room, and he came running over to me, and I saw an animal with eyes that were beautiful, life-filled, and laughing. Teddy is now the dog with laughing eyes.

(August 17, 2005)

A RATHER NICE DREAM.

Last night, I dreamed I died. It was a rather nice dream, actually.

I was sitting at my desk, writing. I typically still write things out longhand, and then type them into my computer later. There's something about the feel of a pen or pencil in my hand, the soft sound it makes working its way across the paper. Something about the way the words look on the page. Something about the way it allows the wording to keep pace with the thoughts.

In my dream, I was just finishing a work. I don't know exactly what it was. But it was something I was enjoying writing. Perhaps a story – maybe one of my columns. I remember seeing the black ink on white paper. And I remember seeing the word "love." That was nice.

When I was told it was time for me to go, I said: "Let me just add a couple of more words, please – I'm just about finished." Yes. Even at this most critical phase of life, I argued with God. But I was allowed to finish my thought on paper. And then my hand was gently pulled away, and the pen scratched unheeded across the bottom of the page. I saw a fading line of ink, wandering softly, and then gone.

It reminded me of when I have been working too long in reality. Usually at my computer keyboard. And Teddy, my newest pal – the German Shepherd mix who has recently come to live here – decides that it is time for me to stop. He gently, but very determinedly, pushes my hand away from the keyboard with his nose. He's quite persistent. He insists that it is time for me to come pet him, or play ball with him and Sophie, or just do any number of things that involve laughter and love and having some "fun." Sophie usually joins him at this point. She brings me her toys and throws them in my lap. Or steals one of my shoes from under the desk and takes off running. It is quite useless to ignore this very compelling beckoning.

And so it was in my dream. I was gently prodded by two angels. At least I think they were angels. I had the feeling that I may have known them. A vague remembrance. But they were the ones who pulled my hands away and told me that it was time for me to come do something that would be much more fun – and full of love and laughter.

It was a rather nice dream. There could be harder ways to pass from this life than in the midst of doing something I truly love to be doing. To die as I had lived, writing messages for my friends, and stories with which they could remember me.

And then I thought of all the other delightful ways that Aiken itself invites me to "come play" in this life. With music recitals and plays, dinner parties and book clubs, horse races and games, grand woods and gentle gardens, long walks and laughter. There is great conversation with good friends. There is beautiful art and charming architecture and wondrous nature. There are a million stars to admire, and a moon that more often than not makes you catch your breath. There are awesome new scents and brilliant new colors every season. And amazing new joys around every corner.

In fact, I have heard many people say when they first move to Aiken, that it's almost like being in heaven. From its warm, personal hospitality to its slow, gracious pace of life to its abundant, ever-changing natural beauty.

It was a rather nice dream. But, somehow, I am inclined to believe that, perhaps when I do get my call to stop writing, and if I do get to step into Heaven, I may turn to God and say smiling: "Why … it's almost like being in Aiken."

(September 14, 2005)

Christmas Arrived Last Sunday.

Christmas arrived in Aiken last Sunday. It came in with a parade.

Up and down Laurens Street, for an hour and a half, we waved and clapped and were serenaded with carols and wished Merry Christmas from a vast array of marchers and floats, performers and fancy cars. There were horses and high school bands, scout troops and politicians, robot-makers and future farmers. There were dogs wearing hats and horses pulling carriages, one giant rabbit and several pretend reindeer.

This annual parade is a very egalitarian event. Most who want to participate can. It's a wonder that anyone is left in town to watch. And yet, there we were, hundreds of us, sitting on curbs and standing on sidewalks, thoroughly enjoying the spectacle that our friends, neighbors and co-workers were creating just for us.

The sun was warm, the breeze was cool, and at the end of the line we were served cookies and sweet tea in the First Presbyterian Church.

I thought to myself that this was the perfect example of all that is good and truly wonderful about American hometowns. And then, there was more.

Following the refreshments, we were invited to watch a special Christmas pageant staged by the children of the church.

Capitalizing on the much-anticipated Disney release of the C.S. Lewis classic, "Narnia," this updated version of the Christian faith was capsulized for us – complete with imaginative costumes and beautiful music and creative sets and scenery. It segued immediately into the traditional historic version. Quick backdrop scene changes took us from "wardrobe" to "stables" in seconds.

This part of the story had it all: live animals, shepherds, angels, wise men, and, of course, the Holy Family. I was in the back, so I couldn't see particularly well, and I have to admit I never did find the baby Jesus. But that was a mere technicality. The rest of the performance made up for it. It was absolutely perfect.

Mary and Joseph in place, the sheep and goats were brought in with the shepherds. The tile floor and an unexpected audience startled one of the sheep, which did what startled sheep will do, and then it began head-butting the shepherds, who promptly got the giggles. The angels – replete in beautifully feathered wings and sparkling halos – valiantly lifted their skirts as they tiptoed through the sheep poo. The young camel had a penchant for kissing and nibbling the actors' hair, causing King Herod to stand on his throne to avoid these amorous advances. A couple of the sheep and goats got a little rowdy at this point, nearly wiping out the backdrop. The sound system was rather sporadic. The room was overly warm. Some actors' lines were forgotten, while goats were ad-libbing, and baby brothers and sisters in the audience kept talking at all the wrong times.

But through it all – in spite of it all – because of it all – it was one of the most beautifully presented Christmas pageants I have ever attended. The children were amazing. They portrayed this timeless story with utter innocence and passion and joy. They filled the room with peace and love. They reminded us all what this season is truly about. And we laughed and cried and hugged each other when it was done. And then we went home with the spirit of Christmas firmly and joyously in our hearts.

Christmas arrived in Aiken this day. It came in with a parade and was told in the voices of children.

(December 7, 2005)

THE CHRISTMAS STOCKING.

It was at the bottom of the box. Carefully folded. Tucked in among the packages that were wrapped in colorful reds and greens and patterns of snowmen and Santas. It was my childhood Christmas stocking.

It had been delivered to me in a brown cardboard box – shipped by my parents who had obviously uncovered it as they continue to "down-size" and dispose of and pass along a family's lifetime of accumulation. There, together with the packages of new surprises and unknown delights intended for opening this upcoming Christmas morning, was the unexpected, well-worn, red-and-white-cloth memory.

My hands reached for it first. I knew immediately what it was, of course, even before I turned it over and saw the familiar script-written "Martha" across the white band at the top. My heart filled with joy and sadness. Simultaneous, spontaneous, tears and smiles. Something caught in my throat.

This wasn't my first Christmas stocking. Somewhere, in an attic-stored trunk I know I could find it. Colors faded. Fabric worn thin, even to nothingness in places. That original stocking had outlines of Santa in his sleigh and candy canes. It was long and thin and held my first blocks and a small cloth doll and, later, a set of jacks, I remember.

But not far into my life, my mother must have decided it would be fun for us all to have matching stockings to hang across the fireplace mantel. These stockings, however, were for decoration only, rather than filling with tiny treasures.

Each of these mantel stockings was made of red felt. Graduating in sizes – from Dad's largest to Mom's to my older sister's to mine as the smallest. A baby-size was added for my little sister after a nine-year spread in ages. Attached to the top of each stocking was a wide band of white felt. At the left edge, there was a cloth loop for hanging. And across the white top band was written in bright red ink, in plain script lettering, our first names.

To me, more than anticipated treats and seasonal secrets, these stockings represented our family. There we were, all together, a "set." Different sizes, different names. But we matched. We were complete. We belonged to each other. Hung across that Christmas mantelpiece every year was red-and-white-felt proof that we were a family.

I don't remember when the red felt stockings were first omitted from the rest of the decorations. I suppose they fell out of fashion after awhile. Or perhaps it was when we began to grow our own families. And we all moved away to different houses, different towns, different states.

As the only daughter without my own family, however, I continued to join the rest for Christmas in their homes. It is great fun to be visiting "Aunt Martha," who arrives in a flurry of snow and presents and leaves too soon. I have been blessed to have shared 60 Christmases with my family – wherever they have been. I have adored doing it, even though it has meant leaving my own home for the holidays for over 35 of those years. Driving, flying, snow storms, ice, in the middle of the night – "I'll be home for Christmas" no matter what.

This year, however, I have decided that I will be "home" for Christmas. I will be home right here, in my own beloved Aiken. It is time that I celebrated in my own home, with my own wonderful friends and loved ones right here in this hometown place. And, when my stocking arrived in a package today, it was the perfect love- and wisdom-inspired gesture from my family.

So, to each of you, my Christmas wish this year is that you have your very own red-felt stocking, a mantel upon which to hang it, blessings and memories with which to fill it, and a family to love because of it.

Merry Christmas. *(December 21, 2005)*

THE FENCES OF AIKEN.

My friend Jeannie is building a fence for me around my front yard. She is an artist as well as a craftsman. And it is truly a family affair. Her husband plants the posts deep and true and perfectly aligned. And sometimes her young son comes along, to play with the dogs, or help carry a board, or just keep us all good company.

She lets me participate by helping with the plans and making all the hard decisions – like choosing the right post caps and the perfect gate latch. We started with a drawing, but have changed and revised as we've gone. And now it is taking shape just as I imagined it, and yet not at all as I had pictured it. So for me, it's a happy collaboration of design and surprise.

Mine is a stained wood fence, with pickets and open spaces and some panels with swoops and cutouts. It angles invitingly at the front gate to ask the visitor to please step in. Another gate at the side has a marvelous arbor for you to walk through as you enter.

It's not a tall fence. Just high enough to keep a couple of rather large-sized dogs tucked safely inside. I envision it someday supporting masses of long-stemmed flowers and sweet-smelling vines – with perhaps a birdhouse or two.

Already, passersby wave and make nice comments. And it confirms my belief that, on the whole, fences in Aiken enhance our inherent atmosphere of long-standing Southern hospitality. Rather than bar your way, our fences reach out to you. They welcome you in to sit and visit awhile, to perhaps have a cookie and a cool glass of sweet tea. These fences create outdoor "rooms" – complete with wonderful views, sweet fragrances, friendly sounds, and fresh air. These fence-sided rooms seem to be a specialty of the South in general, and of Aiken in particular.

Even the grand old houses, the ones that have "Old Aiken walls" surrounding their properties, have wide, inviting grilled gates – usually left open wide. And most have lovely flowers and plants cultivated on the outside as well as within. These outdoor rooms have been made especially for leisurely lawn parties and afternoons of croquet, charity flower shows and favorite granddaughters' weddings.

I have smiled at a few of the Aiken fences I've seen. There are those with low holes cut out just the right height for resident dogs to poke their heads out and watch the world – and maybe to also let a visiting pup peek in. And there is at least one fence I've noticed that is obligingly cut up and away from the ground a number of inches high and wide simply to allow a big old tree root room to be. Like Grandma with a cutaway shoe in deference to a bunion.

One neighborhood gentleman that I often see as I walk the dogs uses his low open-brickwork fence to test his golfing skills – up and over and into a vacant patch. And then back again.

Some fence walls are solid and low enough for children to walk along the top, practicing balance, steadied with caring parents' hands. Others are vine-covered masses of green – the fence itself lost from view long ago. And, of course, many Aiken fences are traditional horse-style – painted white or black planks, just low enough to let horse noses be petted over the top or to say "hey" to the riders or stable folks.

Fences in Aiken do, I believe, simply enhance the ambiance and tradition of genuine hospitality and friendship here. They define within them spaces of solitude. But solitude that is meant to be shared.

"Half the pleasure of solitude comes from having with us some friend to whom we can say how sweet solitude is."

– William Jay, 19th century American philanthropist

(March 1, 2006)

Obedience 101.

Her name is Sophie. She's about 17 months old. She's the mixed-breed puppy I found and brought home to live with me a little over a year ago. Sophie is a gorgeous redhead, with goofy ears that flop on the top of her head, big fat feet, a long flowing tail, a heart the size of Canada, and a vast appreciation for silliness. All of Sophie's indeterminate ancestry must have been on the large side. She's well over 50 pounds.

For her own safety (and mine), I decided we needed to go back to puppy school. I say "back," because we attended a few classes about 6 or 8 months ago. And Sophie excelled – blew those other puppies out of the water. But Sophie thinks of obedience training rather like a performance art. To her, it's something that she should do only during class, in front of an audience. She finds it difficult to realize that this behavior is supposed to continue at home – to be an actual lifestyle change.

Sophie also believes that "close" is good enough. If you're commanded to "sit," and then you get bored, you can also lie down, roll over, stretch out on your back, and try to get the other dogs to look at you. To Sophie's way of thinking, the command "down" includes crawling on your stomach to your closest classmate and poking them with your nose, or creeping along on your tummy over to something you might want to check out in the grass. "Sophie, come!" can actually mean, "whenever you feel like it … or be sure and chase those pesky birds and check out all the bushes along the way." The word "heel" is just irritating and a distraction from the real meaning of a good walk.

Sophie and I attended our first class a few weeks ago. For that initial session, I left Teddy at home, and took Sophie only. Teddy is the German shepherd-mix I found and brought home about 6 months ago. After living with sweet and lovable Teddy for these past few months, I thought that taking him to obedience school would be a bit like training a lima bean. Teddy really doesn't do much. He has rather perfected the art of slowly doing very little. I thought perhaps I could home-school him. What I hadn't anticipated, however, was that leaving Teddy behind would break his heart. He pouted for days.

The teacher is wonderfully understanding, and is now allowing Teddy to "audit" the class. It has also been a terrific help to have had a close friend visiting for the past few weeks. He takes Teddy and sort of walks him through each class, while I concentrate on really getting the points made with Sophie.

Each week, Sophie is getting better and better at her lessons. And I am getting better and better at practicing everything at home with her (perhaps the real meaning of obedience training). We're about half-way through the course, and I can see a definite difference in Sophie's behavior, as well as in our relationship with each other.

Surprisingly, there has been a difference in Teddy, too. He's somehow more confident now. He acts more like he "belongs." It's like he's "in with the in crowd" in his mind – allowed to sit with the popular kids in the cafeteria. He doesn't have a clue what any of the commands mean, of course. But he genuinely appreciates being included.

In the midst of this sacred season of Easter, I can't help but make some connections between the lessons my animals have been learning – and what they are teaching me about my faith and spiritual understanding.

Through them, I am reminded of some of the basics: Come when you're called. Mind the commands, even when you don't understand why. Don't walk ahead of your master. Stay put and listen sometimes. Keep practicing. Include everybody. This is not a performance art, it's a lifestyle.

May you and your family – animals and all – enjoy a beautiful Easter together.

(April 12, 2006)

Porch Lights.

I must have been very young. Maybe five or six years old. I could barely see out the back seat window of the family car. But whenever we happened to be traveling at night, I used to watch very carefully just to see all the houses with their front porch lights on. There, in the deep purple night, or the soft gray dusk, was a glow of yellow warmth. A beacon. A light put on just for friends or strangers.

I remember thinking that these houses looked so inviting, so welcoming, so friendly. And I would wonder sometimes about the people who lived there. They were always "families" in my young mind. Happy families with lots of love and plenty of food. And a dog.

Of course, my own family always had lots of love and plenty of food and a dog. So this was probably my prototype. But, to my youthful imagination, these glowing houses with front porch lights on had these important elements ready to share. Thus, the porch light. These were the houses that were lighting the way for someone to come to the door. Inviting people in for dinner. Letting someone know they would always be welcome to come there if they needed something. A home that offered unquestioning hospitality.

Sometimes, a particular porch light would wink just at me. And I would wave back. A small wave. A secret just between us.

It was a long time ago in an age of innocence. I was an age of innocence. It was a time and place when people looked out for one another. Offered help even before it was asked. It was the youthful perception that families were always loving and homes were always safe and strangers were always welcome. And all of this could be told by a simple soft light shining on a front porch.

I vowed to my five-year-old self that, when I grew up and had a house of my own, I would always keep the front porch light on, too. Perhaps it became a symbol of happiness to me as much as hospitality. And, when I did grow up, and I did have a house, I did leave the front porch light on. For awhile, anyway.

Then, over the years, I began to forget sometimes. And there were years of living in apartments and three-floor walk-ups that had no front porches at all.

And then, I moved to Aiken.

I began to notice just how many houses here in Aiken still leave their front lights on. Not only on porches, but down walkways and drives and at corners and gates and entrances. How lovely and warm and inviting they do look.

How perfectly Aiken. This place that is always so open to new friendships; this town that goes out of its way to welcome a stranger; these neighbors with kindness and good will and Southern charm so ready to share.

And so, I have rediscovered my passion for this simple expression of happiness and hospitality. I have begun again to leave my front porch light on. It is in the midst of a whole neighborhood where almost all the other homes do the same.

So, perhaps one soft summer night, a family will drive past. And a little girl in the back seat will peek out the window. And my house will wink back. And she will wave.

(May 10, 2006)

Peace and possibilities: horse training in Aiken.

The early morning sky was the color of stainless steel with a thin veneer of clouds stretched across it. It had rained all night. The ground was puddled and mud-slicked. The air was damp, almost chill.

Few incentives will compel me out of bed before 7:00 a.m. on even the brightest of Saturday mornings, but this invitation did so. A friend of mine owns a share in one of Cot Campbell's horses. Cot is the well-respected long-time force behind Dogwood Stable here in town. He is the man who originated the business of syndication or "partnerships" within the thoroughbred industry whereby people can own shares of a racehorse. Share the costs, share the risks, share the benefits. A simple yet brilliant concept. It lets people who are less than millionaires still enjoy being a part of this fascinating world and invest in all its "possibilities."

My friend recently retired from a self-owned business. The proceeds from its sale were her lifetime savings. And with them, she then realized a lifetime dream by buying a share in one of Cot's horses. A beautiful bay filly, full of curiosity and potential. With an unrelenting taste for peppermint.

This particular Saturday morning, we were going to see the filly "breeze" – an industry term for asking her to run flat-out – on Aiken's Training Track. She would be among a handful of other horses doing the same thing. It was worth the early hour, I decided.

It was with disappointment, but not surprise, when we were greeted with the news that track conditions that morning would prohibit them from performing this ritual with safety. So instead, the horses would be allowed to trot and put in an extensive gallop for us.

Several owners of several horses were there. And Cot, Ron, Mary Jane, and others from Dogwood. Exercise riders, hot-walkers, grooms. We all mingled and talked – about horses, of course, and the weather, and good places to eat breakfast now that the track kitchen had closed for the season. And we talked about the next step for these equine athletes in training. About how most of them – my friend's horse included – were leaving within the week for more training and then racing at faraway tracks. Exciting, yet somehow sad.

Together, we all crossed the road to the training track and stood on the clocker's stand. Two-by-two, the horses were trotted and galloped in front of us, then came jogging back for us to view them again. The animals were patently obvious in their awareness of us – watching us, wondering about us, perhaps showing off a bit for us. Eventually, we all returned to the stables. Here, we watched as the horses were unsaddled and bathed and walked and cooled. Then they were turned out in the paddocks to eat sweet fresh grass and have a good roll and visit with one another before they were stalled again. It was so peaceful and calm. Quiet and comforting. Only kind hands touched the creatures with patience and caring. Only soft voices spoke to them, about them.

I thought back to a time early in my writing career when I had been assigned a story about a Futurity Stakes Race at Churchill Downs. I was allowed behind-the-scenes access on the backside. I was a part of the hustle and noises, the crowds of people and horses, loud trucks and huge barns. All the hurry-and-wait bustle and atmosphere that saturates such a place. And I considered these young Aiken horses. Would they adapt? Would they draw strength from the calm and kindness of their Aiken beginnings? Would they perhaps even learn to thrive in the energy-based rhythm of those tracks and their races?

I suppose I considered, too, how I have come to Aiken at the other side of my own career. I have already run my first races. I have come in from "out there," with hard-won experience and only a few minor injuries. So I relish this community of peace and patience and pace. I welcome its courtesy. I am energized by its quiet safety and kindnesses and character.

I have decided that I will look forward to seeing more young horses work out at dawn, as they are cared for with quiet excellence, as they grow into their potential within this insulated community. And I will be sorry to see them move on. But I will hope for them to realize all of their promise. And I will hold a good thought that they will always remember the peace, protection and other values they knew while they trained here in Aiken.

(June 7, 2006)

YES, BARBARA, THERE IS AN AIKEN.

Over a hundred years ago, Francis P. Church, the editor of the New York newspaper the Sun, penned the words: *"Yes, Virginia, there is a Santa Claus,"* to reassure an eight-year-old girl about the existence of this symbol of Christmas joy and love and goodness. It became a beloved work – and a classic phrase defending an ideal in the midst of a skeptical, imperfect world. Recently, I had occasion to recall it.

Last week, my parents visited me here in Aiken for the first time. I was thrilled. I couldn't wait to show them everything. All the beauty and charm and character of this amazing place I love so much. I wanted to have them see and hear and experience firsthand all the wonderfulness I have discovered about Aiken. In fact, I had been sending them my columns about my life here regularly – sending them to all my family and friends – rather like fond letters home.

I began their visit here with a drive down South Boundary – a street like no other. They were properly inspired. And then they remarked, "Oh, we'll have to tell Barbara about this." And they took pictures.

Next, we walked down Laurens Street and Newberry – and they held hands. We ate in a small café. And they said to each other, "We'll tell Barbara about this." There was a concert in the park. Well-tended stables with playful young horses. Old architecture and curving brick walls. Beautiful fountains and lush flower gardens. An ancient forest in the heart of town. Sweet tea and sweeter Southern hospitality. Each experience resulted in their utter appreciation … and the same ultimate comment about conveying the message to Barbara.

Barbara is my older sister. I also have a younger sister, Pat. To date, neither of them has been able to visit me here. So I keep sending them my columns and photographs and telling them all about my new hometown. But my parents were the first to come here to experience it for themselves.

Finally, several days into their visit, I had to ask, "Why do you keep saying that you'll have to tell Barbara about everything you see and do in Aiken?"

They answered, "Well, Barbara doesn't actually believe in Aiken."

"You mean, she doesn't think it exists?" I responded. "Where does she think I live?"

"Oh, she knows it exists. She just doesn't exactly believe all the things you write about it," they replied. "She doesn't think any place can be that good."

"What about Pat?" I wanted to know.

"Oh, she believes you."

"So … does Barbara know that what I send her are actual columns – that they actually appear in the local newspaper?" I questioned.

"Oh, sure."

"And, does she think they would print those columns if I were just making all this stuff up?"

"Mm. Good question."

As a final gesture, I booked us all on a tour of "Historic Aiken" under the guidance of Judith Burgess. Judith's family has been in Aiken for generations. It was perfect. She took us from street to street and told us story after story and pointed out history and folklore and added personal remembrances and insights. At last, everything I had been telling my family since I first moved here seemed to be proven and verified and witnessed.

As we stepped off the trolley, I said, "So, now you've heard it from an expert – and you've seen it for yourselves. It's all true, right?"

"Oh, absolutely. But of course, we always believed you, dear." They patted my hand reassuringly and said, "And now we'll tell Barbara."

Mr. Church wrote in his editorial to Virginia that Santa Claus exists just as certainly as love and generosity and devotion exist. That he exists to give life its highest beauty and joy, an opportunity for childlike faith and poetry and romance. In his words: *"Alas! How dreary would be the world if there were no Santa Claus!"* And Virginia believed.

So to Barbara, I hope you now believe me. Because, alas! How dreary would be the world if there were no Aiken.

(June 21, 2006)

SHE LOOKED AFTER THE LOSERS.

It was a small plaque, only about three inches high by five inches long. It was attached to the back of a simple wood and wrought iron park bench, standing alone along the path at the far east side of Hopelands Gardens. I don't know why it caught my eye. But there it was. Perhaps the sun dappled across it just right. And there, engraved on it were the words: "She Looked After The Losers."

I was out walking the dogs, Sophie and Teddy. Too hot to walk anywhere else. But wonderfully shady and cool and quiet in Hopelands in the summer. A private retreat, a shared privilege. Usually, Sophie can't wait to watch the fountains. Teddy must see the ducks. We tug anxiously along the brick-lined pathways. This day, it was a slower pace somehow. I saw it as we passed. "She Looked After the Losers."

Her name was also engraved upon the plaque above the statement: Anne Choate Dodd. I didn't recognize it. I don't know anyone of that surname. And yet, I knew something of great importance about Anne Choate Dodd: She looked after the losers.

My walkmates would not stop for long. Ducks to the right. Fountains to the left. But the words came with me. They tumbled through my head for the rest of the evening. I loved the straightforwardness of them. "She looked after the losers." In our politically correct society, it was refreshing. She did not look after the disadvantaged, or the people who made wrong decisions. She looked after the <u>losers</u>. The ones that <u>lost</u>. The ones who <u>were</u> lost. At least she considered them as having tried. You can't lose if you don't try. I also appreciated that she "looked after" them. It was active, personally involved, but not condescending. She didn't just care about them. She also didn't take care of them. She looked after them – a subtle difference. And also somehow a very

Southern way of phrasing it. Anne Choate Dodd looked after the losers.

I came back the next afternoon, too. I wanted to see it again, write it down exactly right. I brought a human friend with me this time and we talked about it. She didn't recognize the name either. We wondered aloud about who gave this bench in Anne's memory. Whose lives did she touch so deeply that they would honor her in such an insightful and honest way?

Fate prevented me from having to search very long for the answers. In a chance telephone conversation, I was told that Anne Choate Dodd was the mother of Anne Campbell, a long-time resident of Aiken, someone I knew at least slightly – certainly by reputation. And it did not surprise me that this woman of character would have been the daughter of another woman of such obvious substance and character.

I learned that Anne Choate Dodd lived a long and very full life looking after the losers. She took her young daughter with her to visit prison inmates and the mentally ill and others who were sick and down and out. She tucked strangers under her wing and supported the weak and gave money to those who needed it and read the Bible to those who needed it. It was just what she did.

She hired a yardman named David who let the lawn fall into woeful neglect and disarray. But when asked, she replied, "Well, honey, you know David's blind."

It wasn't until the daughter was well into her teens that she one day challenged her mother's approach to life. With innocent logic and sense of purpose, her mother responded, "Honey, somebody has to look after the losers."

Anne Choate Dodd suffered her own deep losses. Life losses that could crumble most of us. But she was forever full of hope, filled with joy and light and duty – looking after the losers.

When Anne Choate Dodd died, her daughter spoke about her philosophy. She built her eulogy around it. She honored her mother's name with her own words. Soon after that, a loving nephew surprised Anne Campbell with the bench in her mother's honor. The tribute was attached.

I know I will go back often now, to that bench on the far east side of Hopelands Gardens. And I will remember Anne Choate Dodd and feel as if I knew her heart. Perhaps one day I will see someone else there, too – reading her legacy. Perhaps it will be someone else's mother, and she will be saying to her own little girl, "Well, honey…somebody has to look after the losers."

(July 5, 2006)

THE CALL OF IMAGINATION.

It's a low, throaty, sort of yowl. It repeats over and over, as many as 10 or 12 times in a row. It can sound rather haunting when it comes in the dead of the night – which it frequently does. It can wake me from a sound sleep, even from the other end of the house. It stirs the dogs, who lift their heads to listen, grumble a bit or sigh deeply, and then curl into a new position at the foot of the bed. It's been happening, off and on, for a few years now. Lately, it's been growing in frequency and intensity. The origin of this mysterious disturbance is my aging, stone deaf, female cat, Katie.

I worry that she has feline dementia. Perhaps she is seeing things – shapes and forms that aren't really there. I hope they're not frightening to her. Perhaps she is calling to kittens long grown and gone. Perhaps she finds herself in a room she no longer recognizes. Or is surrounded by sights and scents she can't quite recall.

Whenever I go to her during one of these "calls," she stops abruptly, and seems to be in no distress or discomfort. She purrs contentedly at my touch. And then I think that perhaps she doesn't even hear herself. After all, she is almost totally deaf. I can also suspect the opposite – that it may be her own private form of "Karaoke night." And that she's simply performing a tribute to the Golden Oldies. Perhaps the tap dance was about to begin. I hope I haven't interrupted thunderous applause from adoring fans.

So I scratch her ears, and whisper words I know she cannot hear, and turn off the light. It will be at least a few more hours before her imagination – for good or bad – takes over her reality again.

I believe wholeheartedly that cats (and dogs) have very vivid imaginations. How else can you explain their ability to dream? Or their absolute abandonment in chasing down a runaway mouse that is nothing more than a sock or bit of folded paper tied to the end of a string? Or how that moving toe beneath the sheet becomes a killer mole?

It makes me recall a quote from painter Pablo Picasso: *"Everything you can imagine is real."* It also brings to mind a recent evening spent at the Nancy Carson Library in North Augusta, in the presence of perhaps 40 children – the source of the most enviable imaginations.

The audience – of many different ages – was treated to a wonderful live theater presentation of "The Frog Princess," performed by a group of students, the youth wing of the Aiken Community Playhouse.

It was, indeed, theater up-close and personal. Some of the little ones, seated on the floor in the first few rows, had to be gently realigned several times, as they crept closer and closer to the actors in front of them. I must admit, my attention was often drawn away from the staged action to the faces and reactions of the children. They were utterly absorbed in the moment. Their disbelief was suspended completely. Their imaginations had become their reality.

One youngster was so convinced of the reality of the moment, that a wooden dagger waved about became a bit <u>too</u> real. And Dad's lap was a much better place for viewing from then on.

For almost an hour, we all believed in magic spells and princesses disguised as frogs and the power of kindness and love. And, perhaps, we all learned an even better lesson. Not simply that imagination can become reality; rather, that perception is reality. *"It's not what you look at that matters, it's what you see,"* is how Henry David Thoreau expressed it.

That night, we all looked at teenagers and saw royalty. Tonight, I hope Katie will look at me and see her old best buddy. I hope her yowls are belly laughs. Or one more chorus of "Hello Dolly." I hope wherever each of us looks, we see love waiting, friendships and possibilities, a prince or two, and cats who love to dance.

(August 2, 2006)

THE LITTLE BOY

THE LITTLE BOY, 1855.

"*The Little Boy, 1855.*" That's all the lovingly carved gravestone says. There is no first name, no family name, no birth date, no age. Achingly simple and small and sad.

The Little Boy's gravesite lies within the Graniteville Cemetery. I had heard vague tales about the mysterious little grave, and I wanted to visit it for myself.

When I first entered the oldest part of this remarkable cemetery, that traces its history back more than 150 years, I was caught by its timeworn, timeless beauty and ambience. Ancient, gnarled cypress trees and wide-spreading pines weep with faded brown Spanish moss draped along their outstretched branches. Well-worn red-clay pathways lead you down passages of time. Stone walls and benches beckon. Peace is everywhere.

Throughout the carefully marked squares of its land, there are still a few dozen remnants of old grave markers made of wood. The names and dates are long lost to the elements, of course. Their fragility is woefully evident. The weathered grain on these stubbled planks are like lines etched deeply down aged grey faces.

The wooden markers are the exception, though. Mostly, there are hundreds of artfully carved heavy stones and large slabs of marble – now black with years, yet still legible with care. There are old, lyrical names written on them, like Lucius and Orlena Mae, Mattie and Samuel and Bess and Beauregard. The headstones are covered with symbology. Marble urns are draped in deep folds of carved stone to speak of unspeakable sorrow. Tall, slender columns represent a life cut short. Doves are for the soul and peace and hope. Small lambs are lying at rest.

Many of the family-dedicated squares and plats and a few single graves are framed and protected by handsome heavy iron fences. A sign of wealth. Now rust-red-and-brown, they flake and stain your fingers when you touch them. But glorious still.

And there are single graves with short carved stone walls on all sides – like cradling arms embracing the soul within. Some are even simple brick outlines. Some so tiny, they catch your breath. There are more than 80 graves of fallen Civil War soldiers here. Their average age, not quite 20.

It was warm and bright, and the shadows of the old trees offered deep cooling shade. A light breeze picked up the late-summer buzz of cicadas and midday songs of birds and bumble bees. Tiny yellow wildflowers nodded. It is a very peace-filled, spirit-filled place.

Then we turned, and there was the grave I had come to see: *The Little Boy, 1855.*

His story is haunting. He was traveling on a train, alone. From where, to where, no one ever knew. He was tiny, frail, and so ill he couldn't even say his own name or how old he was. Too ill to travel any further, the railroad personnel decided, so they took him off the train at the Warrenville/Graniteville station. He was gently transported to the Graniteville Inn, where he was cared for with great tenderness and compassion throughout his last few days and nights. When at last his little body gave out, the town buried him with as much attention and concern as if he had been a local favored son. With no known mother or father or proper relatives to mourn him, the town adopted him as their own. And grieved his short life and passing.

I had brought a handful of homegrown flowers for him, picked as a last-minute thought from my garden. I laid them at the foot of his tiny resting place. I placed them in the only spot I could find. For it was overflowing with flowers and toys, stuffed animals and crayons, and all the treasures a child of any age would understand and value. I saw a Pez dispenser. Miss Piggy and Kermit. More matchbox cars than I could count. Colored pencils. Pennies. A miniature plastic dog. A small rubber snake. Little folded notes. A large, blue marble. For more than 150 years, this grave has never been without such gifts, from countless unknown visitors – children in particular.

The story of "The Little Boy" could break a thousand hearts. Instead, it has touched them with hope. The children, most of all, can see that – in their infinite, innocent wisdom. They know instinctively the ultimate truth. That "The Little Boy" died far too young and far from home is not really important. That he died *loved* is.

(September 13, 2006)

A TAPESTRY OF ROOTS.

The trench had to be dug. It was the plumbing. The entire system – from house to cottage to street – self-destructed (in the middle of the night, of course). So the trench had to be dug. Across the driveway (twice), through well-established bushes, past one ancient oak, one magnificent magnolia, and under the lovely herringbone pattern of a vintage brick patio.

The workers are being quite careful and conscientious and sensitive about the wake of destruction they seem to be leaving. And they promise no long-term harm will come to the living things they're nudging aside. They'll put it all back, they say. (Well, almost all. I get to recreate the brickwork myself. It's a good thing I like puzzles.)

But the trench that had to be dug is gaping and deep. And ever so compelling to dogs and cats (quite "cool," actually). Even I can't keep from stooping under the yellow caution tape and carefully walking along the piles of earth on either side, peering into the new chasm that awaits the modern-day pipe.

It happened as all plumbing problems do – at a most inconvenient time. It is unbelievably costly to remedy. And it was inevitable with an older home. Less than six months ago, I wrote lovingly about the joy and mystique of owning an older home. I must re-read that column to myself again a few more times.

It was no longer a choice of repair. It had to be replaced entirely. And so, the digging began last Friday and continues as I write this column.

The workers have gone for the day, and I have joined Sophie and Teddy in gazing at the newly created valley that now laces my backyard. The earth still smells newly turned. It is darkly facing upside down in mounds on either side. But what I am most in awe of is the thick latticework of roots that is revealed – that permeates the walls and floor of the trench itself. Most have been cut away, but many still stretch out to the other side, like fingers reaching across to lace in silent prayer. Some are as thick as tree branches themselves. Others are like long, thin harp strings. They weave around and over and under each other in a sort of loving, living tangle.

The workers say the thick presence of roots slows the trenching progress, but they are careful to trim away only what is necessary. To do otherwise would weaken the trees and bushes, and cause the beauty above the ground to falter – perhaps to die.

What a metaphor for my beloved Aiken, I think. Generation after generation has created this rich tapestry of roots – a history that runs deep, but is also just under the surface, and still connects us through the living, breathing, evidence above. This is our strength. Our heritage. It is what supports the beauty we see and experience all around us – the sweet blossoms and the unique character of this place.

Perhaps some trenches do have to be dug – to repair and replace, to reinforce, to keep life flowing. But where roots are strong, and where care and integrity are used in the digging, beauty and character still bloom – as lovely as ever, rich and deep and sweet, for generations and generations to come.

(March 28, 2007)

THE EASTER PARADE.

It was, indeed, a proper Easter parade. There were fancy bonnets and flowers, streamers and floats. Antique carriages and carts. A grand procession of finery and fun. But last Saturday afternoon's parade in downtown Aiken featured primarily a host of decked-out doggies. There were horses as well (this being Aiken) – some of them tiny miniatures. And a couple of extremely opinionated cats. But the day belonged to the dogs.
An SPCA special.

It was a fine day for a parade – especially one made up of furry creatures of all sizes, ages and descriptions. Warm in the bright sun, but a cooling breeze to ruffle floppy ears and tails.
A fine day.

I took my two canine friends to watch: Sophie the redheaded mixed breed, and Teddy the German shepherd mix. I told them all about where we were going. But, of course, what they heard was "car." A word filled with anticipation nonetheless.

When we parked and got out of the car downtown, it was again a moment of wondrous possibilities. There were so many people and other dogs and kids who knew how to pet gently. There were smells to smell, and soft wet noses to greet, and tails that said "hello" with enthusiasm.

Everyone was walking and waiting and looking up and down Park Avenue, anxious for the parade to begin. And here it came!

"Sophie, sit," I commanded, "Teddy, stand." (Stiff back legs supersede the sit command for him.) Sophie reacted immediately and her eyes grew big as the horse-drawn carriages passed right in front of us. Teddy was facing backward, so he missed that part.

People waved and called out our names. Many even commented on how well behaved Sophie was, sitting so calmly. I didn't bother to tell them that she was probably rather overwhelmed with awe and thinking if she sat very still, no one would notice her.

Teddy still hadn't determined which way to look. Apparently the crowd behind us – or perhaps it was the store windows – seemed to be most amusing. His tail was still pointed toward the parade. "Turn around, Ted," I encouraged. But his feet remained firmly planted.

I had to laugh as the assorted canine Easter bonnets of the parade marchers became tilted across an ear or had slid down the participant's back. Many were worn more as ascots than hats. But the idea was there, the festive appearance undaunted.

Sophie never moved. Her ears stayed close to her head. She was fascinated, but intimidated, and sat tightly next to my legs.

"Teddy, turn around, dear," I kept coaxing. "Look at the doggies…see the horses. Hey, Ted, *cats!*" But Ted was in his own unexplained world. Enjoying the backside of the parade route. Could he be watching the reflections? I wondered. Or maybe it's a silent "protest" against dogs in hats. (On second thought, that would be a bit sophisticated for my dear Teddy-boy. And probably an unlikely gesture from a dog who wears a cardboard birthday cone on his head with an elastic string under his chin for hours and seems to enjoy it.)

It was a short parade. But exceedingly fun. Full of as much joy for the participants as it was for the audience.

As we wandered slowly back to the car, I kept wondering what Sophie and Teddy had made out of the whole experience. Was it something they would remember? Was it fun for them, too? Why wouldn't Teddy turn around?

Then I thought perhaps it's like most things in life: some of us are participants, some of us are observers, and some of us simply let the parade pass us by.

(April 11, 2007)

KATIE THROUGH THE LOOKING-GLASS.

Katie spent most of last night trying to step through the large dressing-table mirror in my bedroom. Apparently, the room on the other side looked terribly inviting – even though it was simply a backhand version of the room just behind her.

Those who read my column regularly may remember that Katie is an ancient, longhaired calico cat who now has feline dementia. Most of the time, she lives in a world all her own. She refuses to stay in the house (letting herself out through the doggy door). She sleeps at the very top of a 12-foot-high brick barbecue. She eats only the left side of her food (I have to turn the bowl around so she can finish it). She rarely recognizes me or the dogs or the other cats who live here. She has very little hair left. She is deaf as a stone and "talks" by way of screeching with a sound and volume that can peel wallpaper.

On many levels, Katie seems to be ready for locked doors and paper shoes. But I hate to impose confinement on her, when she still seems to be quite happy. Physically, she's in relatively good health. She's safe within the walls of a large backyard. She eats well (from the left). And seems to enjoy life as she defines it. Another point in her favor is that we now live in the South. And the South has long treasured its eccentrics.

Last night, it was pouring rain. Katie did not realize it. So I had to physically remove her from her outside perch and try to convince her to stay in the house. She first became obsessed with eating the other animals' food – but, since it was just the left-side portion of it, they didn't seem to mind. Then, she compulsively kept sticking her head into a square box of Kleenex. I was never quite sure whether she was trying to climb into the box itself, or if she wanted to shred the tissues within, or if she simply enjoyed the sensation of having it engulf her head. It seemed harmless enough and amused the dogs.

By bedtime, I had coaxed her into the room in which I sleep, and had tried to take her into bed with me. It's the way she used to sleep for most of her former life. But, at first, she would have none of it. She didn't know who I was, and was quite suspicious of me. With a flying jump (belying her age and stiff joints), she gracelessly went from the bed to the dressing table top. Bottles and brushes and other items went sliding and crashing to the floor. But she managed to land safely, body-slamming against the large round mirror that creates the back of the unit. Looking deeply into the reflection, she decided the "other" bedroom was a much nicer place to be. She butted her head against it, scratched at it, yelled at it. Over and over. With the infinite patience of the deranged. She was determined to reach the other room.

I tried waving at her, turning her around, showing her it was just a reflection. But she refused to be swayed. That was the place she wanted to be.

I wondered what it looked like to her. What did she see that was so compelling? Was it softer in light and color somehow? Was it "familiar" to her in some way? But Katie's mind is known only to herself. Her perceptions are unique. And her perceptions are her reality.

And then I thought that perhaps that is all any of us really need to know about life. Life – our reality – is simply a reflection of what we see in it for ourselves. As Tweedledee said in "Alice Through The Looking-Glass" … "If it was so, it might be; and if it were so, it would be."

Perhaps we can all choose to see what we see – and it will be.

(June 6, 2007)

THE NEXT GENERATION.

Something moved on the other side of the gnarled old Magnolia tree. A flash of white. Figures moving. Faint voices. Then "clack-clack" – wood against wood. Somehow, I recognized that sound.

My two canine companions, Sophie and Teddy, were walking with me. It was our typical morning route, which includes a worn dirt road on the wooded backside of the Green Boundary Club. As we approached the Club grounds, I could see bits and pieces of the croquet field that is permanently maintained across the back lawn of this gracious property.

"Sophie, Teddy, wait," I asked just above a whisper. We slowed our steps and rather crept up to a clearing in the shrubbery and trees that define that edge of the Club grounds. Here, we watched silently the scene that was playing out before us.

Everyone was dressed in traditional whites. Young people, who looked no more than 10 or 12 years of age, were paired with gray-haired instructors. They were learning the art of the game of croquet. Rules were carefully explained; techniques were patiently practiced. Quietly. With appropriate dignity. But not without giggles. There were spectators sitting unobtrusively in painted wooden lawn chairs at the sides of the field. It was a gentle step out of time. And it made me catch my breath.

"It's the next generation," I thought. "A new generation of civility and tradition."

The lawn itself was cool green and glistening in the morning sun. It was well-rolled into its required level playing surface. The children listened intently, respectfully. The elder players were kind, obviously enjoying the passing on of this centuries-old game to the younger ones.

I know that the Green Boundary Club is only about half a century old, but croquet was brought to the United States shortly after the Civil War. Aiken, the genteel sporting capital of the time, would have been a natural playing ground, embracing the game's challenge and history. Croquet itself can trace its roots back to an even older form, enjoyed in the 17th century in both England and France. But its great popularity in the late 1800s and early 1900s would have assured its inclusion in Aiken society.

Aiken's love of sport is legendary. Its pure joy in the outdoors is well known. Even its apparent appreciation for the equality of the sexes on fields of competition and in sporting events is well documented and remembered. So, of course, croquet would be present here. And exceedingly well-loved.

As I stood there in the shade of the ancient trees, and watched through the thicket of leaves, I felt as if I were looking down a tunnel of time. And yet, I was particularly grateful that it was here and now and in the present. Because this was a glimpse of truth that I hold dear. This was, indeed, the next generation. This was a new generation learning to keep at least one more moment of the past – one more aspect of graciousness – alive and well and living in Aiken.

(June 20, 2007)

Good shoes and Southerners.

"Y*ou've seen these shoes before,*" she said with a smile. Mark Fox at Fox Shoe Repair nodded and picked up one of the shoes, turning it over slowly in his hand. It was a delicate dance shoe, champagne colored, an intricate pattern of glass beads covering the toe. It looked incongruous in the man's hand, which was large and muscular and browned like the leather he works with on a daily basis.

She reminded him that he had dyed the shoes once before – to their current golden champagne. Now, she needed them to match a soft fawn-colored bit of material that her daughter handed him across the worn glass-and-wood counter. He assured them that it would be no problem and that they would be ready on Tuesday.

I had just given Mark a shoe of my own. One of my favorite sandals. I had told him I didn't care what it looked like, I just wanted to be able to keep wearing these comfortable old friends. I don't remember when or where I got them. But they have been with me a rather long time. He had said the same to me as he was repeating to the woman and her daughter with the fancy dress shoe. Sure, he could do it. They would be ready on Tuesday.

It was my first time in the shop, and I had been lingering longer than I needed to, drawn to the pungent odor of tanned leather and oily shoe polish, as well as the sights on the surrounding walls and shelves. There are the expected offerings of assorted shoe polishes and laces. There are other types of leather goods for sale, too – wallets and coin purses. Mark says he doesn't make them. But he knows the guy who does, so he carries them. To the left of the counter, there are bottles of old-fashioned food flavorings: vanilla and almond, lemon and black walnut. On a countertop to the right, there are home-canned preserves of strawberry and applebutter and peach. Mark's mother-in-law puts them up for him to sell. Hanging on a couple of walls at the other end of the store are old posters featuring John Wayne, "The Duke" he's called on them. And high on a wall behind Mark is a row of stuffed foxes. Not exactly to my taste, I have to admit. But Mark says the kids like them. He used to keep them on the floor in the old place for the kids to pet. But there's not enough floor space in this new location, he explains. There is barely room for a row of old chairs along the front window for the weary shopper. I have to smile at their seats of worn, cracked, unrepaired leather.

Another woman enters the store to pick up a large attractive purse she has left to be repaired. "I just love this thing," she says to Mark. "I'm so glad you could fix it. I use it all the time." Over the course of the next few minutes, two more customers come in to pick up and drop off shoes for repair. I don't know why their shoes are special; they didn't say. But they'll be ready on Tuesday.

Fox Shoe Repair is in its third generation; its second here in Aiken. Mark's uncle started the business. Cousins run additional stores in Augusta and other places. Mark learned the trade and then took over the business from his dad, who took up the craft during the depression.

Mark's soft voice, slow smile and unhurried hospitality fit right into my growing feeling that Fox Shoe Repair seems to epitomize one of my favorite things about Aiken and the South in general. True Southerners value what is good and keep it. True Southerners appreciate quality; they savor it; they save it. A true Southerner uses grandma's china, chips and all. Crystal glasses glitter just fine after being washed by a couple of generations of hands. Sterling silver shines even deeper with decades of buffing and polish. Old homes exude grace from behind rose gardens planted a century ago. Both only need loving maintenance to bring continuous comfort and beauty to the families that dwell within them and the community to which they belong. Both are passed with great care from one generation to the next.

So, I suppose, in the spirit of true "Southern-ness," good shoes get repaired. Old purses get new life. And well-loved dance slippers are re-dyed for yet one more ball. And I suspect that, thanks to good shoes and Southerners, Mark Fox and his family have heard the words: *"You've seen these shoes before,"* more than once.

(July 18, 2007)

Fox SHOE REPAIRS
"LOOK NEAT, START WITH YOUR FEET"

Tennis, polo, kings and presidents.

"1066," he said, as we leaned back in our chairs in his comfortable living room. "William the Conqueror. South of England." And then we both had to laugh.

I had begun the conversation with this fascinating gentleman by asking him to tell me his family story – starting back as far as he wanted. But 941 years ago and a continent away were a bit farther than I had anticipated we would be going. He was explaining how his family name had come into being. And, "Ashhurst," in old English meant grove of ash trees – a place (and name) that had been awarded to the family by William himself in 1066 for their loyalty to the British ruler. "I had an aunt who always told me to never associate with anyone who dropped the second 'h'," he went on to explain about the spelling of the name.

Fred Ashhurst has lived one of the most interesting lives I believe I have ever come across. All nine-plus decades of it have been interlaced with historic local, national, and international events and people and places. And he remembers it all in colorful detail.

Mr. Ashhurst was born and raised in Aiken. His father had come here to work for the original Mr. Hitchcock around the turn of the last century. A chance meeting in a railway carriage had led to the Aiken legend inviting the young man to relocate here and help him with his business affairs. In his childhood, Fred Ashhurst remembers if he was a "bad boy," he had to work in his father's office, running errands and performing other small tasks. I didn't ask what being "bad" might have involved. But it resulted in his crossing paths with some of Aiken's most remarkable citizens from a very early age. Mrs. Hitchcock and her son Tommy were among them. Through Tommy, he recalls having met Eddie Rickenbacker and some of his other WWI compatriots – known colloquially as the "Hat-in-the-Ring" boys.

His youth is filled with Mead Hall and The Citadel, tennis games and polo, dances in Charleston and falling in love, and of meeting Will Rogers. I got to hear about President Roosevelt and Lucy Rutherfurd – "They were very much in love," he commented. He talked of a beautiful mountain laurel named "Kalmia" growing on the northside of town, and the first car brought to Aiken, and how his brother learned to be an auto mechanic because no one else at the time knew how; about giving tennis lessons to the Kennedy boys in Palm Beach ("liked Joe very much, didn't care for John"), and about joining the 7th regiment of the National Guard in the second world war (they were known as the Silk Stocking Regiment because of their perceived affluent backgrounds); and about a boy named "Whistle" who took a phone call from President Roosevelt that sent another Aiken man to consult with the Commander-in-Chief about entering the war – a full three years before the country was actually committed. There were tales about the New York 400 (families of unprecedented wealth and influence), most of whom wintered in Aiken. I saw a picture of an Aiken man who had courageously survived the sinking of the Titanic, and heard the infamous story of another who had disguised himself as a woman to gain access to a lifeboat (the latter being ostracized by an outraged Aiken community thereafter).

Fred Ashhurst was born in the oldest house in Aiken at the time. He knew that Dwight D. Eisenhower would be asked to run for president three days before Ike himself received the news (an Aikenite did the asking). He grew up with the family who had the largest library in the area. He once refused to allow Nicky Hilton access to his own father's hotel tennis courts in the Virgin Islands (where Ashhurst was tennis pro) because the young man refused to wear a shirt. His best friend was the poorest boy in town who grew up to be Chief of Protocol under President Nixon. His next-best friend was a beloved dog name Millie who was too smart to be involved in politics.

It amazes me to realize that I have lived approximately two-thirds the amount of time that Mr. Ashhurst has – but haven't had even a fraction of the experiences. Of course, very few have. If anyone wonders about Aiken's place in the history of world events, Fred Ashhurst is living proof of their reality. I am deeply privileged to have spent even a few hours in his company.

Right now, Fred Ashhurst is thinking about collaborating with someone to write a book based on his memoirs; I call "dibs" on him.

(September 26, 2007)

Wish you had been there.

I'm sorry you couldn't be with me. It was your kind of day.

Lightly tinted clouds domed the field and held back the heat as well as their rain. A stiff breeze kept the humidity at bay, and mingled the assorted scents of horses, leather, smoky bar-be-cue and expensive cologne.

This was the second year I have been to an Aiken polo pony sale, both times without you. It was the ninth hosted here in recent times. I can well imagine this same scene out of Aiken's history. It would have been fun to see if you thought the same.

Over the last century and a quarter, polo has been a continuous, integral part of Aiken and her culture. Nearly as long as the sport has been played in this country. And, not many years after its introduction here, an enterprising father and son relocated to Aiken specifically to raise and train horses for polo. Surely their sales must have resembled this tradition-filled event. View, trial, anticipation, celebration. The integrity of the seller. The grace of the bidder – win or lose. The dignity of the pony. The unpretentiousness of the participant.

One of my favorite aspects of the sale was watching the auctioneer. His dance with his right toe and gavel, keeping pace with his lips and tongue as he calls and cajoles the bidding with dizzying song-like syllables, until the final bang and pronouncement of the winner. Seated next to him was the "color commentator." This man describes each pony and its potential; defining the perfect buyer; challenging the bid to reach its maximum. "A steal!" he calls out. "An absolute steal!" after one seller accepts a closing bid.

In front of them are the bid-takers. Serious men. Dressed in coats and ties. One wears a straw hat. Their eyes flash across the crowd, constantly moving, watching. They know the real bidders, although I could never see who it was making the nods. The bid-takers' hands signal the auctioneer with practiced assurance. Silently communicating, remembering who and what and where and when.

I try to recognize the buyers. I think it may be the ones with designer haircuts and perfectly fitting coats. The women in pearls. The men with a hint of South American gracefulness about their walk and casual charm. But perhaps they are the ones who have the most muck on their boots. And sun-colored skin. And callused hands. Perhaps they are both. A very egalitarian affair, the polo sale.

And then, there are the dogs. I love the dogs. Some pure, some mixed. Some friendly, some less so. All share the same attitude of entitlement. One pup seems unable to refrain from hanging around the front of the auctioneer's stand. In charge of the horses – indeed, the entire activity – as only a Jack Russell can be. But no one seems to mind. Least of all the horses. You would have laughed at the dogs.

I didn't stay too long without you. I refrained from sampling the food (although it smelled mouthwatering). I talked to just a few of the sellers, as they kept back behind the crowd, only a little distracted. The serious buyers were too busy to chat. Catalogues twisted into cones and well marked in black pen and tucked with a bit of secrecy under an arm or in a back pocket.

I walked away and looked at the polo mallets for sale and other equipment, and at the original paintings of horses, and then at the out-of-state cars parked at the edge of the field – Tennessee, Texas, Colorado. Once again, Aiken draws from across the sport and across the country with its acumen and atmosphere and excellence. I left reluctantly. But I promised to bring you ice cream and sympathy.

I'm sorry you couldn't come with me. I'm sorry you had the flu. But what luck for us both that we now live in Aiken, where the joy and experience of ponies and horses of every kind are here all year long. You'll be there next time.

A get-well message to my friend, Barry.

(October 10, 2007)

THE CHILDREN OF AIKEN.

Her tiny hand was plump and warm and slightly sticky as she reached out and put it into mine. We were both sitting on the edge of the Newberry Street fountain, watching dogs in fancy costumes as they paraded across a makeshift stage.

I heard her mother warn her that if she fell into the water, she would be taken home immediately. She looked up at me for a quick, calculating moment. Then she stuck out her hand for mine. An invitation I couldn't refuse. Although I was a stranger to her, I was apparently found worthy of being her guardian against the dreaded threat of falling into the fountain. She never spoke a word, nor did I. It was a simple bond of trust.

She wasn't more than three years old. And, on this day, she was a purple unicorn. More padding than substance. All blanket-like softness. A tiny round face and dark curls peeking out from one end, small well-worn shoes from the other.

It was Halloween and "Trick or Treat on Newberry Street" in downtown Aiken.

In addition to the doggies on parade, we were surrounded by witches and warlocks, pirates and princesses, bride dolls and superheroes. There were a few little pumpkins and long-eared pink rabbits. A bee or two. At least one cowboy. The majority, however, were primarily dress-up and face paint and imagination. It made me smile.

Suddenly, I was back in my own long-ago youth, where hobos and ghosts and brown paper sacks were the mainstream of Halloween costumes. Dad's old shirts and mom's hats and long gloves. Cowboys and Indians. Old newspapers fashioned into sailor hats and pirate swords.

It brought back even more memories to see that about half of the parents on Newberry Street were into the spirit of the night as well, wearing costumes or silly hats themselves. I remembered one year when my mother dressed up in a heavy coat and mask as she walked the neighborhood with us. A very short woman, she was unanimously mistaken for one of us kids – to her great delight. At house after house, she was offered candy and treats along with the rest of us, until she got the giggles and gave herself away.

This Halloween party in Aiken wasn't confined to Newberry Street, of course; the merchants throughout downtown welcomed the revelers with handouts and hospitality. Shoppers and dinner patrons gladly made way.

But what touched me the most, I think, was the overwhelming atmosphere of a shared experience. A shared experience that had at its center the welfare of the children. Youthful excitement was gently surrounded with parental care. And grown-ups were even a part of the game. Children were free to roam and pretend out loud, because we were all there to watch over them. A village raising a child.

This was, indeed, a night of sharing – imaginations as well as sweets. And age and income and background had no part of it. It was simply a family having fun together. Including the family dog. It was one soft, warm, slightly sticky hand holding another.

(November 7, 2007)

BEAM ME UP, VICKY.

Their names are Violet, Vicky (I'm told its Victoria, actually, but her friends call her Vicky), and Maggie-the-Cat. They are three, glossy, well-spoiled, very black, cats. And they live with Ellen at "Beam Me Up" used book store.

On Park Avenue, just east of York, just to the left of the SPCA Thrift Shop, there is nestled a perfectly musty, wonderfully jam-packed, old shop thickly lined with worn, loved, previously owned books.

I discovered it quite by chance. A unique three-wheeler parked out front, its rear basket filled with paperbacks, first caught my eye. Next to it was a table of funky old costume jewelry. Pins and bracelets and clip-on earrings. I spotted Violet the moment I stepped through the doorway. Her sisters were curled nearby. Ellen introduced us.

The pungent smell of old books has always drawn me closer. And the immediate impression of confused disarray I found charmingly compelling. Slowly, however, the scene before me began to take on a bit of order as I scanned the book titles. Romance. Mystery. Science fiction. They were generally grouped together according to contents on wide wooden platforms and table tops. Children's books and stories about animals. Biographies and chronicles of war. Collections of photographs, stark and haunting in the black and white of their historical importance.

There are rows upon rows of old cookbooks. Do our tastes really change so much? And there are dusty text books that haven't seen a classroom or desktop for generations; still smudged from the grasp of young hands now grown old. Their titles are almost illegible. Faint, scrawled pencil marks in the margins document the challenges they once posed.

There are record albums from the 1960s, and sheet music from pre-World War II. A catnip-filled sock peeks out from under a stack of books about dogs. A framed photo dated 1946 hangs slightly askew above paperback collections of gothic castles and women of courage waiting to be rescued.

I stopped short and smiled in front of a murky vase filled with dead vines. Crisp and brown. Not a trace of life left in them. But they seemed oddly appropriate here – somehow perfectly at home among these volumes that are so alive with voices waiting to speak to us from across decades of life's experiences.

There are more odd pieces of jewelry – perhaps someone's gift on a long-ago Mother's Day or birthday or a token of Christmas love. A few stray cups and saucers and plates. A frame or two. And more books. Everywhere, more books.

Ellen, the proprietress, is perfect in her role. Tiny and bright, she somehow knows exactly when to talk you through better understanding her system of book stacking, and when to leave you alone to explore for yourself. She's there to help find a title for which you may be searching, but never seems to "hover" intrusively.

I picked up a biography of Mussolini. A heavy thing, both in content and size. "I can do better than that," Ellen said, as I looked at the very reasonable price inside. In fact, she "did better" on every piece I bought that day.

In the end, I came away with the weighty biography just mentioned, a small volume of my favorite novel "To Kill A Mockingbird," a recent fiction called "The Last Templar," a 50-year-old reprint of William Faulkner's "Sanctuary," and a 1946 edition of "Gentleman's Agreement" (later adapted into a classic movie staring Gregory Peck). To this assortment, Ellen graciously added a delightful book about a dog who saved cats, after we got to talking and she discovered my passions.

Ellen and her partner started the shop in 1994 (she has continued alone since her friend passed away more than a half-dozen years ago). The intriguing name "Beam Me Up" came from no more exotic a reason than she has always liked the original TV series of "Star Trek."

I wonder how I could have missed discovering this quirky delight until now. But Aiken is like that, I've found. Consistently offering new treasures to uncover just around every corner. And on this day, my gem was waiting down Park Avenue, past York Street, to the left of the SPCA Thrift shop, and providing an utterly perfect backdrop for three black, silken beauties named Violet, Vicky, and Maggie-the-Cat.

(November 22, 2007)

WAITING WITH THE BLUE HERON.

The ancient, gray skeleton might never have come to light, had it not been for the excessive drought this past year. Not of human origin – or even animal or bird or amphibian – it is the bare bones and underbelly of the Carolina Bay that has been exposed.

Tucked away on the southern edge of Aiken's city limits, this is a favorite walking place for me and the dogs, Sophie and Teddy. It stunned us to see it so barren and suffering and vulnerable. I knew the Bay itself was becoming more and more shallow over the weeks and months without any meaningful rains. But I was not prepared for the empty reality that greeted us on this day's walk. It had been awhile. And, like visiting an old friend who has been struggling with issues of health or other life stresses – a friend you haven't seen for too long – the change made me catch my breath.

The lone, large, resident Blue Heron was still there. Standing regally and aloof as always. But, today, he was out in the very center of the Bay. Posed erect on a mound of smooth gray clay that jutted unexpectedly into the air. I had never seen this island before; it had always been well beneath the water's surface. Only a few segregated areas of ponding water remain. Enough to reflect some of the flaming reds and golds of the trees that surround the Bay in refuge I noted. It is usually one of the awesomely beautiful autumn panoramas I look forward to in Aiken. But the greater part of the Bay's surface is now undulating gray earth. In some places, a soft covering of green grass-like growth sprouts up. It looks a bit like the delicate strands that typically wave across the floor of a wild pond. Young spring in color. Hard to place. Out of place. In other areas, where the clay has dried and is beginning to harden, there are a few footprints – both animal and human. Perhaps they crept forward into this foreign ground out of curiosity. Perhaps, as fellow mourners, they came to pay their respects.

I remember when I first saw this Carolina Bay. It took my breath away then, too. But for entirely different emotions. It had been a very wet season then. The Bay was at its peak of intriguing, natural loveliness. Full of life. It was celebrated on Earth Day. The water was like a liquid mirror, reflecting the sky and branches of its forest, rippling from small life forms within and above. Birds gathered to praise it. Creatures hovered near it with sounds of delight. It was pure magic. And I wrote a sort of loving tribute to it in one of my early columns. Its beauty and mystique utterly convinced me that it was created, maintained, and inhabited by "The Fairies of the Carolina Bay."

Now – today – the fairies seem to be in hiding; hauntingly absent. The birds are silent. No ripples dip the small, dead pools. Only the lone Heron waits.

Even the sky has begun to shed a light mist of grief over this almost forsaken place. Sophie suddenly jerks up her head in anticipation. But it is only a fallen leaf tumbling uninterrupted across the open space.

The mist has grown heavier with promise now. It clings in tiny droplets on the needles of the pine trees. It makes the gray floor slick and shiny. Perhaps there is hope for its reclamation, I pray in my heart. For all the living things that have loved and left here, I pray for the rain in my heart.

I know that the Carolina Bays are millions and millions of years old. I know they have survived countless droughts and floods and years of erosion and the interference of man for generation after generation after generation. I know that this, too, shall pass. It will be reborn. And, even in its altered state, it is somehow incredibly, compellingly, lovely still. It continues to be a place of absolute magic.

Sophie and Teddy and I will try to be hopeful and wait. We'll wait for our beloved Carolina Bay to come back to us. And, for a few minutes today at least, we crouch low and sit – in sadness and hope, in silence and mist. We sit and we wait. We wait with the lone Blue Heron.

(December 5, 2007)

Teddy got his butt blessed.

Teddy got his butt blessed on Palm Sunday afternoon. It was a lovely ceremony. Not the blessing of Teddy's hindquarters, per se. But the entire Blessing of the Animals that was hosted by First Presbyterian Church in downtown Aiken. It was an inaugural event for the church, and one I personally hope will continue on an annual basis.

The sun was warm on the west lawn of the church. There were folding chairs and blankets spread on the ground. People came from every direction and every denomination. There was music and cool refreshments, prayers and celebration. It was a very spiritual experience.

Those who came to be blessed were mostly dogs of every description, a few slightly startled cats, at least one gold fish that I knew about. Everyone was quite congenial and reverent. There was a deep sense of peace throughout the gathering. So I'm not sure why Teddy refused to willingly participate.

There had been heavy storms the night before, and he continues to be deeply affected by some past, private terror related to such weather. Perhaps he was still wary from it. And the music was live. And there were strangers all around. And Sophie, my other canine companion, was quite the social butterfly and perhaps not as attentive to him as he would have wished. I had to be away from him during much of the event, too – helping to serve communion and other duties. So his solution was to make himself as tiny as possible, and climb backwards under my folding chair. His tail tucked tightly against his body. His limbs curled against himself. His head down. Pretending he wasn't even there. Only his backside protruded from the front of the seat ever so unobtrusively.

After the singing and prayers and special remarks, the humans were offered communion. Walking immediately behind the servers, the minister for the event, Holly Shoaf-O'Kula, came to each animal and blessed him or her individually. First one row, then the next. Touching each creature personally with love and tenderness. Asking God's blessing on each small soul.

Sophie accepted her blessing with a light heart and happy spirit. Then, it was Teddy's turn. I could only glimpse bits of what was going on, as I was serving communion and focused more on the duties at hand. But at Teddy's chair, the minister paused longer than usual. She was kneeling on the ground. Coaxing. Encouraging. Gently prodding. But Ted was refusing to respond.

Ever since I took Teddy in to live with Sophie and me about two years ago, I have known that Teddy is going to do what Teddy is going to do. He has come a long way from his early days of abject fear and mistrust. But he will, at times, retreat into himself and simply refuse a new experience. Often unexpectedly. Always irretrievably. This was such a moment.

I am grateful to Reverend Holly for her persistence, and ultimate acceptance. She simply blessed what she could reach of him. And Teddy got his butt blessed.

Perhaps we are all "Teddys" at some times in our lives. Perhaps we, too, refuse to leave our hiding places, our comfort zones, our self-designed invisibility. And, in doing so, I wonder what delights we forego, what blessings we miss receiving?

I hope we are all fortunate enough to have someone in our lives who will coax us, encourage us, prod us. And, when all else fails, who blesses our butts anyway.

(March 26, 2008)

MONDAY MORNING COFFEE IN THE COMPANY OF MEN.

I've always enjoyed being in the company of men. Both singly and collectively.

Men have a distinct way of thinking and feeling and looking at the world, it seems to me. They have a unique process of relating to each other as well as to women in general and to individual women in particular. I sincerely appreciate the gender as a whole and, as stated earlier, being in their company.

So it was with great personal pleasure that, a few Mondays ago, I was allowed to sit in with the Aiken Downtown Coffee Club. All men. Invitation only. This was quite a privilege.

I was advised to come around 11:00 a.m. The members actually get there about 10:30-ish, and, I was informed, this would give them time to get their coffee and tell each other lies and jokes and stories about the week before. Naturally, I didn't want to miss any of that stuff, so I got there well before 11:00.

My "in" was Carl Langley. He and I had met a few years back during an author signing at the library. The wife of a newer Club member also played a key role in getting me invited. (This is no easy party to crash.) Even the place where they gather to have their coffee is kept somewhat to themselves. And they've moved the location a few times over the years, although the reason behind these changes rather depends on whom you ask.

Carl has been a member for about 20 years – not an actual founder of the original group, he is currently its semi-official appointed leader. He can also easily tell some of the best stories. Some are about his experiences as mayor of New Ellenton. And his years writing for the Aiken Standard. And about some very interesting characters he's known along the way. (Although Carl himself might qualify for one of the more intriguing personalities.)

Most of the members had been advised that I was coming, so I was met with gracious hospitality. The majority of the men are from the era and upbringing that still lifts him to his feet when a woman enters the room, and leads him to gently take her hand with an introduction. I even got a hug or two from a few acquaintances and husbands of friends. These were truly Southern gentlemen, no matter where they were actually born. This morning, there was Carl, Jim, Bob, Steve, Malcom, Frank, Dudley, Al, Dick, Ed, Dave, three Joes, and Charlie. Charlie's just a part-time member, though. And Ronny was in the hospital.

The stories were fast and smart and continuous with several running jokes. I was only able to catch bits and pieces around the two tables. Not nearly enough. I was told some grand tales about a dead mule on Millen Street and unsolved murders and surviving surgery (there was chewing gum involved). There were also remembrances about family histories that reached back to the very founding of Aiken. There were personal experiences from W.W. II, and more recent international history making. And, of course, obligatory observations about politics and the economy thrown in for good measure.

Everybody ponied-up a dollar for the coffee. You get it for yourself in a paper cup, I learned. (Although I was duly treated and personally served.)

There was a great deal of intelligent conversation and laughter and kindness all around, and then, all too soon, the men started to wander off, one and two at a time. On to their days' activities. They carefully bid me goodbye, put their chairs back neatly under the table, and disposed of their own paper cups. All too soon, I had to return to the ordinary things of my day, as well.

I realize that this was probably my one and only time to sit in with the Aiken Downtown Coffee Club (they have another, unofficial, name for themselves, but I was sworn to secrecy and it wouldn't be printed anyway). But I'd like them all to know how much I appreciated even this small glimpse into their gathering. I hope they keep it going for several more generations to come.

I do, indeed, enjoy being in the company of men. And these were some of Aiken's most charming examples. But I also never forget the Ralph Waldo Emerson quote: "Men are what their mothers made them." I suspect wives have an influence, too. So, to all those involved: Good job, ladies.

(April 10, 2008)

BUNN
Omatic

THE DOG IN THE AIRPORT.

Mushroom was her name. A sweet, mannered, flirt of a girl dog – mostly pug, with another breed mixed in there, too. A welcoming heart on four legs, with a come-scratch-me tummy, a tail with a twist, and ears edged in black that flapped happily against her warm round brown face.

She stood politely amidst a small pile of luggage and her owner's legs at one side of a long busy airport concourse. Having been too long away from my own pets, and having a layover with some potentially boring discretionary time, I asked if I could make her acquaintance. Both she and her human agreed. She, with unhesitating glee.

She immediately offered me a squeak toy to share. It was so new it still had its tags attached. Great fun. And how generous, I thought. How dog. To be so willing to share something that you, yourself, had barely had time to thoroughly explore and enjoy. Pure, instinctive, honest hospitality. The "dog-share" principle.

For these first few moments of introduction, my focus was entirely on Mushroom. Dogs first, humans second. Nothing new. It's who I am. But above my place on the floor with Mushroom, the human's voice was cordial, his laugh sincere. His delight in my appreciation of his companion was obvious. A lovely shared connection.

I looked up into a pair of very blue, shining eyes above a smile that was warm and genuine. The rest of his face was simply not there. Skillful reconstruction had obviously been tried. Thick makeup attempted to cover the scarring. Perhaps it was a devastating fire. I guessed at his age -- perhaps it was war related. But his eyes were bright with humor. His smile warmed my heart. And that's all I saw for the rest of the encounter. Nothing else seemed to interfere with our mutual love of animals. Mushroom simply took our minds away from unimportant issues.

Other travelers then began to stop and talk with us as well. We discussed particular canine breeds. We talked about the joys and difficulties of traveling with animals. We shared stories and experiences. We laughed and took turns petting the playful pup's soft back or rubbing her tummy or tossing the toy for her. Mushroom entertained and greeted us all. She created easy bonds.

Too soon, I had to move along to catch the next flight. A hug for Mushroom. A handshake and steady smile into the kind blue eyes of her human. The others stayed on a bit. Lingering in shared enjoyment.

As I walked away, my heart filled with gladness and awe at the magic that a single small dog can bring to human sensibility.

Under different circumstances, I could imagine the man alone, unnoticed or ignored. Perhaps – probably – stared at with curiosity. Eyes quickly diverted. No smiles exchanged. Certainly no words. No opportunity to have heard his lyrical laugh and seen the beauty of his eyes. Only the devastation would have been noticed. Only what was missing. Not what was there.

But what was there was Mushroom. Unconditional love. A soul that does not judge. A spirit that responds simply to kindness and a gentle touch. It was she who brought us together. All of us. Different races, backgrounds, ages, destinations. A diversity of faces, and one without. All of us far from home; yet, suddenly, none of us alone. We came together in a moment of easy companionship. We came together simply because of one small, brown dog named Mushroom.

(April 23, 2008)

Embracing change, as well as dogs.

Sometimes change creeps in on four, soft, black paws. A wagging tail sweeps across routine, stirring it into something unfamiliar, almost chaos. A wet black nose prods existing habits into new odd shapes. Relationships are out of balance. Reality as we know it shifts. His name is Sly. He is an exuberant black lab mix. He is living in my house.

Sly came here suddenly, out of need. His human mom was hospitalized on a moment's notice. Then rehab. Finally, a move out of state into the care of family. That was over six weeks ago; Sly is still living with me.

Sly is a "leader dog." Highly trained, very valuable. He has a full working life ahead of him; he has a purpose to fulfill with affection and intelligence. Although he can no longer live with his former "mom," he will be reassigned to someone yet to be met. A new love of his life awaits him. But first, Sly must go back to the organization that will reassign him. It is in Detroit.

Getting Sly to Detroit is not proving to be a simple matter. But it will all work out, somehow, I am sure. This complexity of issues and efforts is not the purpose of my column, however. What I want to tell you about seems wholly more significant.

It's about change. More specifically, it's about the change that Sly has brought to life at my house over the past month and a half. The Sly-shaped impact that has left its impression everywhere.

I am the only human living in the house. But there is Sophie dog, my redheaded best canine pal. And Teddy, Sophie's own personal dog. There is Katie cat, ancient at 19, and in and out of reality, dementia knocking at her door. And there is Sparkey cat who loves flirting with dogs, avoids other felines entirely, and believes he is a species unto himself.

Into this mix came Sly. Sliding sideways, grinning from ear to ear, demanding, commanding, insecure, taller than everyone else, cracking jokes, cutting in front of the line. He ate from everyone's bowl without saying please. He gulped up gallons of water without a thank you. Toys were discovered, reveled in, and mercy-killed. Beds were commandeered. This is mine. This is mine. This is yours, but I'm using it.

Please don't misunderstand. Sly is a good, good, boy. A grand heart. A gentle soul who has no idea how big or intrusive he is. He is a giant spirit of play on four legs. He is a dear dog. But he brought change into our lives as big as he is.

Sophie adapted. She taught him how to play properly. And when. And just how hard to jump and tug (she gives him "time outs" and serious scoldings if he oversteps the bounds). She graciously readjusted her own status in "the pack" to allow for his needs. Walking, eating, sleeping, guarding, "mom time" – she conceded to him full participation rights.

Teddy has been slower to adjust. It is, after all, Teddy. Teddy still shouts at Sly to settle down, and to let him play too, and reminds him that Sophie still belongs to him – that she is still his queen. Teddy does not know his own pack status any more and acts less sure, reacts less happily overall. And yet, Teddy will cuddle with Sly when they are both sleeping. Only Teddy understands why, I suppose.

At first, Sparkey stayed under the house for days. But now he seeks out the added opportunity for Sly kisses and a good ear snuffle.

Katie still recognizes Sly's presence with new surprise everyday. Out of sight, out of reality for her. Sometimes, she stands directly beneath the big black dog and still doesn't really know he is there.

And for myself, I admit I have had less patience than I would have liked. But I have laughed a great deal more, too. I spend twice as much on dog food, and get three times as much protection and affection.

Sly is, quite possibly, the sloppiest drinker of any animal I have ever known. I pile towels around the bowl, and still he flings water all over the floor. At one point, I became almost angry – and then I heard the rhythm he was slurping – to the tune of the old Beach Boys' song: "Ba-Ba-Ba – Ba-Barbara Ann, Ba-Ba-Ba – Ba-Barbara Ann…". It made me start to giggle and so we sang it together and danced.

And thus, lately, I have begun to see Sly not simply as a dog needing my temporary care – but as a lesson in meeting change. With examples all around me, I have seen so many variations of response. Acceptance. Resistance. Hiding from it. Oblivious to it. Cost as well as benefit of it. Bringing out the worst in us. Finding the best in us.

In final retrospect, I think of one of Sly's most prominent habits – demanding hugs on a regular basis. Perhaps this is my lesson to learn to embrace change, too. Perhaps it is simply to overlook the spillage in life, to listen for the music, and to enjoy impromptu dancing with wet bare feet.

(July 30, 2008)

THE MUSIC STILL ECHOES.

There are four paws fewer at the dance now. One less dish to fill. One less leash to hold. One less heartbeat in the house. One less tail to step over in the night. Sly is alive and well and living in Detroit. Sly, the black lab leader dog, who was on sabbatical at my house for almost seven weeks, has reported back for duty. He's getting his act polished, his training refined, preparing for reassignment. A whole new future awaits him.

Two weeks ago, my column told about Sly's impact on my life and home. It celebrated the "joy on four legs" that Sly personifies; and it talked about how intense he can sometimes be. It concluded with how he was helping all of us in this family (canine, feline and human) to learn the art of embracing change in our lives.

I also mentioned in the opening of the column that Sly needed to get back to Detroit, but that it was proving to be a bit of a challenge to get him there. So many had tried to help. So many kind hearts. But nothing was working out.

Then, just a few hours after the column appeared, a woman's name and phone number were forwarded to me from the paper saying she was offering to personally drive Sly home to Detroit. Emotions tugged at me: utter delight that this person would come out of nowhere with such unselfish motives and resolve my dilemma with the perfect solution; yet my breath caught at the idea, knowing that he would no longer be a part of my daily life. And what did I know of this stranger who would be taking him so far away? It wasn't long verifying her complete sincerity, kindness and reliability. She was vouched for by many, praised by all. Sly would be safe in her care, I was reassured.

Sly loved her at first sight. That, too, was reassuring.

I took him to church that night. Wednesday night supper. He would be allowed to say his "goodbyes" to those he had known almost every Sunday and a good many Wednesdays for more than a year as he had carefully led his partner or lay quietly at her side. He had never been able to physically touch or be touched by these other folks before – always working, in harness, on duty. But that night he made the rounds, licking hands and cheeks, accepting belly rubs and ear scratches with simple joy and remembrance. He understood, somehow. Thursday, he spent the night with his soon-to-be traveling companion, and slipped effortlessly into her routine as well as her heart. And then, on Saturday morning, it was time for him to leave.

Sophie and he had one last romp. A final lick to Teddy's muzzle. A backward glance at the cats. He gleefully loaded into the back seat of her car. At least he was going in style, I thought. Red Mercedes. Looking good, Sly. I hugged his neck just a bit longer. He looked into my soul. I waved, and turned to cry.

Inside the house, Sly's silence was everywhere. But the music we danced to together still echoed. The rhythm he brought to our lives was almost audible. I'll try to keep the tune playing in my memory for as long as I can.

Sophie stretched her legs. Teddy picked up a stray ball, then let it drop. We are three again, they know. (Cats not counted.)

In just a day and a half, Sly's "driver" had brought him safely to his destination. She described for me his delight at seeing his old stomping grounds. The recognition and friendship that met him at the door. He knew where he was, she said, why he was there. He was ready to get back to work. She had bonded with the boy quite thoroughly, she admitted. But, of course, let him go with grace and best wishes. And the knowledge that one more person in the world had loved him, however briefly.

This amazing lady got back to Aiken just 13 hours later (a woman of stamina!); and, a few days after that, we had dinner together – the guest of a mutual friend. We discovered fun coincidences in our lives, common ground and mutual likes, shared thoughts and beliefs and loves. We talked of Sly.

I walked away from the restaurant with a new friend. A new sister of the heart. But what kept singing through my mind was a passage from Hebrews 13:2 of the Bible: *"Do not forget to entertain strangers, for by so doing some people have entertained angels without knowing it."*

That will forever be Sly's song, I think. Because of him, I had, indeed, entertained a stranger. Because of him, that stranger turned out to be our angel. Sly's very own angel unaware. An angel named Nancy Mulcahy.

(August 13, 2008)

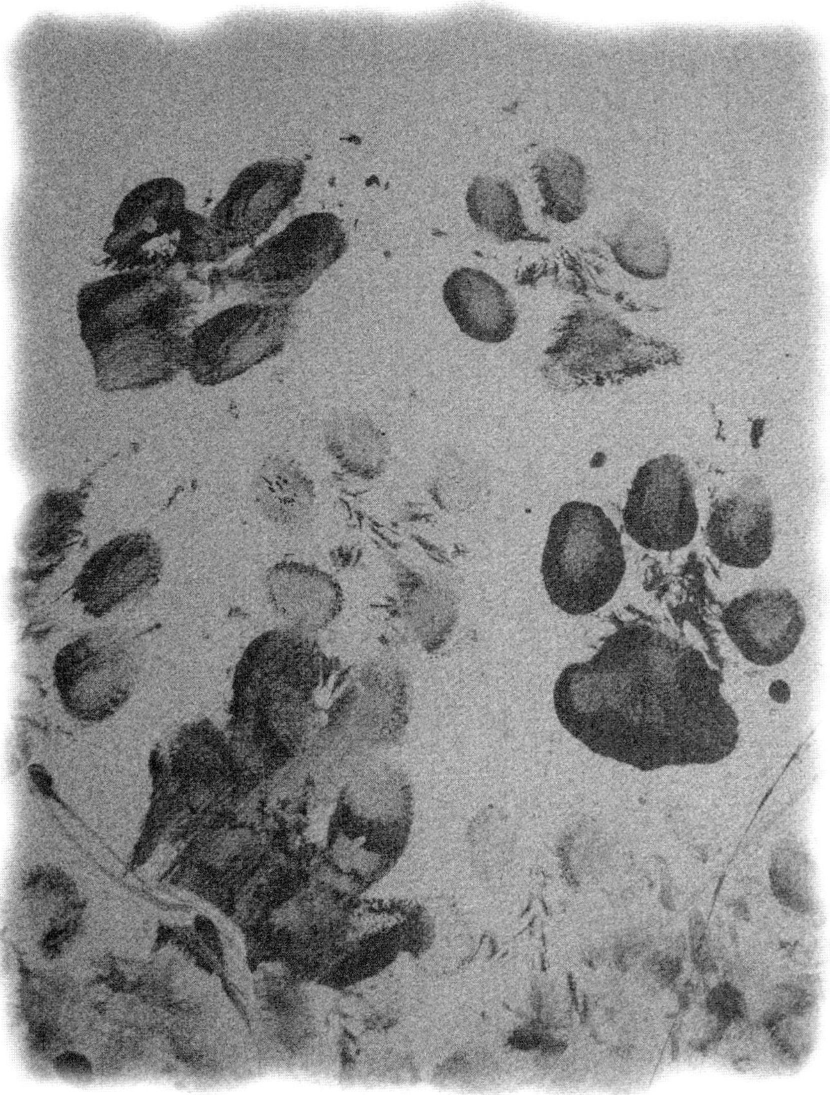

A PUMPKIN OF POSSIBILITIES.

He was a solid little puff-ball with legs. A well-fed, well-confident, little dog. Friendly. Curious. He looked at us squarely and said "hey" in his doggy language sort of way. He stood four-square on his sturdy trunk legs, his chin up and forward, his eyes sparkling.

Under normal circumstances, we would have simply stopped and chatted. We've met before. But I had to laugh out loud at our little greeter today. Even Sophie and Teddy led with cautious sniffs and inquisitive eyebrows. The little puffball dog was cream soft white above, but dripping dark mud below. A perfect half-and-half. He had obviously found a world-class mud hole nearby and had recently enjoyed a good long soak. By his prideful attitude, I could further surmise that his owner had not yet caught sight of him. For this bundle of fun, the day was still full of freedom and wondrous possibilities. He trotted away with purpose – an invitation to follow flung over his shoulder.

The neighborhood in which we were walking is a bit off our normal pathways. The dogs and I try to mix it up sometimes, blending familiar with a tad of adventure and new sights and smells and sounds. These particular streets are a jog and a bend and then a few more blocks out of our customary way. It's a real neighborhood – where dogs can find mud puddles and cats saunter casually from porch to porch; where basketball hoops are set up along the edge of the street, knowing that traffic won't be a problem. We particularly enjoy walking this neighborhood because of the unpretentious yet delightful cottages and plantings and trees one can find here. And, of course, the plentiful animal life. And sometimes even a small carriage to pass us by. And once, a storybook tea party out on a lush green lawn.

On this day, just as we came around the south side of a tree trunk, just beyond the hedge, there it was: Cinderella's pumpkin coach. At least it was the "bones" of it. Unmistakably pumpkin shaped and human sized. But still mostly plywood and screws and unfinished edges. But, oh yes, it was definitely a Cinderella coach in the making.

Sophie, Teddy and I stopped in our tracks in the middle of the street. We gaped and smiled ear-to-ear. I said to the very un-godmotherly man working on it: "Cinderella's pumpkin?" He answered, "Yep."

"Very cool," I responded. The un-godmother's name turned out to be Harvey – a talented crafter of stage production elements among other things. But this was for a private wedding he said. (Well, of course it would be – for Ella and the Prince, I reasoned.) He was creating it for a friend, he added.

The craftsmanship was amazing. His skill and effort went way beyond the bippity-boppity-boo brand of building something. And the joy it would ultimately bring would certainly be as much fun as any storybook tale.

Standing there, I studied it for quite a while. In the end, I realized the real symbolism of the pumpkin isn't the proverbial "happily ever after." It isn't about princesses and princes and perfect lives. The pumpkin, I believe, simply represents the "possibilities." It's made up of good thoughts and dreams, lots of help from amazingly true friends. It takes you to the edge of opportunities ... but then it drops you off to make things happen for yourself. And it doesn't wait around forever.

A Cinderella Pumpkin may be all mystical and magical and founded on impossible dreams. But it also takes ordinary mice on rides of grandeur. It is hope at its highest. It represents promises kept. It depends only on belief and goodness and the innocence of hearts.

And, every once in awhile, it can be found in the middle of an unexpected driveway, just around the next tree trunk, on the other side of the hedge, in the heart of a town called Aiken. Just follow the mud-bellied dog. *(September 10, 2008)*

WHAT ANNIE REALLY NEEDS.

For years we've walked past her house. She was tall and elegant. Snow-white hair peeked out from beneath a yellow straw hat and wisped gently down her back. She was always sweeping or raking the immaculate lawn and drive in front of her house. Slowly, deliberately, always in solitude.

It was my redheaded dog, Sophie, she spoke to first. She admired Sophie's coat as it glinted in the sun. There was an occasional offhanded pat to Teddy's head, too – my less flamboyant tan and brown other mixed-breed canine companion. Her greeting to me came last.

As the months went by, she told me her name: Annie. Sometimes, I would see her walking past my own street. Her arms strained with drooping, heavily laden bags of groceries. Rarely, she would allow me to take one of her burdens from her. Pride usually prevented it. We talked of small, unimportant things, but with great politeness.

Once, she left several books on my doorstep. Wonderful, hardbound classics. She left them, her note said, in repayment for the birthday card I had slipped into her mailbox. (One of the heavy bags I insisted on carrying for her contained a bottle of champagne. It was her birthday, she had confided to me.) She felt compelled to repay me for the small card. But her note said I was not to thank her for her own generosity.

And so, I honored her obvious desire for privacy and independence. She continued to sweetly pet the dogs as we passed by, and speak courteously and quietly to me.

One day, Annie fell. A stroke, the doctors think. She lay alone, on the ground, hidden behind her house, for several days. Fortunately, she was discovered by caring neighbors. She was able to recover mentally, but not physically.

In an attempt to regain her sense of lifelong independence, Annie left the care facility. Even with in-home professional care, she struggles daily with pain and immobility, loss of control and lack of privacy.

For reasons known only to herself, Annie has reached out only to me. For reasons known only to God, I have struggled with my response to her.

Then, one day, I took Sophie and Teddy to visit her. She greeted them with such joy. At just the sight of them, her face was transformed. At first, Sophie hung back, lingering in the doorway. But Teddy never hesitated. He walked over to her bed, immediately climbed in, and lay down next to her. He carefully, gently, touched her paralyzed side. He rested his head next to hers and sighed with his soul.

All of us have Annies in our lives, I suspect. We may struggle to understand their needs. Perhaps we fear their burdens. And yet, I now also suspect that perhaps the most important thing we can do is follow Teddy's wise example: just climb in and lie quietly at their side.

(September 26, 2008)

Laughter in the Labyrinth.

Sophie heard it first: lilting laughter floating on the soft morning air. She raised her head expectantly. Her ears were pricked on top of her glossy red head. Sophie and Teddy – my faithful canine walking companions – and I were in one of our favorite spaces for our daily routine: the paths that weave and bob and crisscross through Hopelands Gardens.

It was the laughter that first caught our attention. Then a few flashes of color seen briefly through dancing leaves on grand old magnolia trees.

It was a final bit of summer. Warm with sun. Just a flit of a breeze. The kind of day that makes me think heaven must have left the back door open.

We began to wander closer to the attraction. As we came up a slight slope, we could see the full scene before us – across a wide expanse of ground and grass, on the other side of some low plantings. Children playing on the labyrinth. There were, perhaps, a half a dozen of them. I estimated their ages to be between four and six. Two mothers were close by, relaxing on a bench.

The children skipped and hopped and danced, all in a line. Perhaps it was a private game of "follow the leader." Giggles seemed a central part of the ritual.

It was the unexpectedness that called to me most. The joy and delight and out-loud innocence that was gracing a place of such traditional quiet introspection. My image of labyrinths has always been a space where one enters into silent contemplation, meditation, wordless communion with nature and God and one's own soul.

The children's laughter reached out to us again, and I was compelled to question why I felt that such purposes must always and only be performed in silence and solitude. I began to suspect that their voices were reaching God's ear quite satisfactorily. And how much more positive would our introspection become if lit with laughing thoughts and the brilliance of just being.

I remember as a child how much I loved to skip. Caught up somewhere between a brisk walk and yet not quite a run, it was, somehow a sort of dance that took you always forward. It was a happy kind of walk, I always thought. Hard not to smile or hum a happy tune while skipping. And, this day, these children were reminding me of that feeling of great pleasantness. A joy of life expressed on happy toes. How perfect it was to skip across a labyrinth.

I know that there is much tradition and wisdom and good that comes from quiet contemplation, silent meditation, solitude and introspection, and walking labyrinths with solemn focus of thought and heart.

And yet, I suspect, we might just try a skip and hop and giggle on our way around it every once in awhile. A child or two or a couple of dogs along might help lead the way. I also suspect the labyrinth in Hopelands Gardens awaits and welcomes either kind of philosophy and traveler with equal relevance and reward.

So if, one fine day, you see a 60-ish woman with two odd dogs skipping around the edges of the labyrinth, please feel free to join right in ... or simply pretend you don't know me.

(October 22, 2008)

ANNIE'S LEGACY.

I wasn't there when the piano was moved from its longtime place of honor against the south wall of the living room. Only the deep impressions on the old blue sculptured carpeting attested to the years it had stood there. I wondered if the piano bench had still contained the sheet music that spoke of her tastes – from classical to Christmas favorites.

The small grandfather clock had also disappeared – soon to be singing the hours and half hours down someone else's hall, becoming part of the familiar background tapestry of someone else's memories of home.

I didn't need or particularly want to be present as all the pieces of Annie's earthly life were sold and dispersed into the community to become enveloped into the lives of others. The estate sale was in good hands. But the night before the opening day of the sale I had walked the house in silence and alone, and looked at all the bins and shelves and furniture and clothes and dishes and books and pictures and other "stuff" that somehow defined her life. Especially the shoes. Annie did love her shoes. And hats and handbags and long kid gloves. Even at 80, Annie dressed with impeccable care. And there were bunches upon bunches of flowers; all artificial; beauty that was never real, but could also never die. Her own personal scent lingered everywhere.

Annie and I were simply neighbors. Passing her house when I walked the dogs, we began speaking to each other – she acknowledged the dogs a bit more than me. But when she had a stroke and fell and became broken and bedridden, she reached out to me. I never will know why. The relationship grew, more from necessity than anything else. But by the time Annie passed away (a few months after her fall), I found myself inextricably involved in her life. These final duties of disposing of her household goods and executing her last wishes have actually given me more insight into the person she was than the time we spent together while she lived. But that, too, was an integral part of Annie, exactly the way she wanted it. Excruciatingly private.

As I was looking over all the bits and pieces and things she had collected and kept and loved over the years of her life, I was suddenly pleased to know that they were being released and scattered out into life, not unlike how her ashes had been scattered to the winds just as she had instructed. And I wondered how different things might have been for her if she had shared herself with the world just as freely before she left it.

Returning home, I walked my own house – both real and metaphorically – and looked at what I have collected and created and kept and found worthy and stored on shelves and in cupboards and closets and perhaps not used to the greatest benefit. Eventually, I went to my books, and finally to the books I have written myself. To a writer, this is perhaps the ultimate act of reaching out and sharing ourselves; sharing our very hearts and thoughts with strangers as well as those we know and trust.

I suspect we all have many treasures stored up in life in bits and pieces, behind closed doors, kept safe for others to enjoy and look at only after we are gone. I wonder at the cause and wisdom of such practices. Why do we not choose to share whatever we can, wherever we can, whenever we can, with whomever we can? And thank God for those who want it, who want us.

And so I thank God for Annie. For her life. For her flowers that will never die. For her joy of music that she has now enabled for others. And for the personal life lessons she has imprinted deeply on the old blue carpet of my soul.

(February 18, 2009)

WALKING WITH GEESE.

Two women walking their pets along one of the dirt roads nestled deep in Aiken's horse district doesn't typically make heads turn. But, just a few days ago, Louise Mellon and I did just that.

It was nearing sunset. There wasn't much traffic. But what little there was slowed, watched, and some even chatted with us. The unusual bit was that, of the eight animals walking behind us, five were gorgeous, white, almost identical, geese. Two ordinary women, two rather short dogs, one timid orange cat, and five amazing white geese.

In reality, Louise Mellon is anything but "ordinary." She nurtures animals and the earth and all those about her in a very special, uniquely quiet, warm, light-hearted way. Her lovely home and grounds are totally organic. She saves abused ponies. She rescues lost dogs. She takes in stray cats. She welcomes the lost and hurting and abandoned, and reclaims their lives with gentleness and love and an open heart. Even her artwork – her painting – is designed to lift spirits and bring a smile to one's soul.

So I suppose I wasn't terribly surprised when I heard about her latest project. The geese.

Then I saw them, met them really, and I was completely captivated. They are still young, only a few months old. But already they are showing signs of the breathtaking loveliness they will grow into. Their feathers are like silk, the softest I have ever touched; a bit of black and grey tinting gives texture and depth to the pristine white of the majority of their down. Their faces hold bright curious blue eyes, and are wrapped in beaks that look like folded satin of gold and pink. Their flat webbed toes and sturdy legs are pale, almost transparent, pink as well.

They are slightly more than knee high, and they want to look at you in the face, and perhaps taste your fingers or a sparkly wristwatch you're wearing or find out what's in your pocket. They talk constantly; a delightful cross between a questioning chirp and the sound a laughing young horse might make. It's a wonderful, gleeful sound.

Louise says they are Sebastopol geese, originating in Europe along the Danube River and the Black Sea. When they are fully grown, their feathers will flow down and out and drape like long, exquisite evening gowns across the ground, and curl and fluff cloud-like all around them. I can see the inherent beauty she describes already showing itself across their supple backs and graceful wings. The fact that they let us touch them and stroke their velvety feathers is such a privilege. And a tribute to their life and upbringing with Louise.

They spend most of their day in the safety of a large, comfortable pen – including their own wading pool and a protective enclosure to run into. When it's time for their walk, they come eagerly to the gate to greet Louise and begin the daily adventure. One is shy. She isn't sure about coming out. But Louise coaxes and reminds her of the fun awaiting her with her brothers and sisters, and she decides to come along after all.

They immediately run to greet me, a newcomer. And I am readily accepted into the gaggle. A welcomed guest.

Down the drive and into the dirt road. We walk slowly, of course, little goose legs can't go very fast and we don't want them to tire or become overheated. When Louise points out a nice patch of fresh grass, they all run to sample it. We wait for a bit, and then walk on, and they come right with us, staying near to our legs, letting us lead the way. The dogs and the cat bring up the rear, of course, as all good and important herding animals should. We don't walk far. Louise knows their limits. Then we turn for home and they come along in complete and easy compliance.

At the end of the walk, they are allowed a few more minutes grazing and exercising through the paddocks and gardens on the grounds. They are utterly agreeable. Amazingly trusting. Genuinely innocent. And perfectly delightful company.

As Louise points out, it's impossible to be sad or downhearted when you are in the company of these lovely and loving creatures. Besides turning heads, they seem to have an inherent ability to simply and charmingly turn hearts.

(August 5, 2009)

Sophie's passion.

It's a special sort of bark. A one-of-a-kind sound from an entire repertoire of voices that my mixed breed dog Sophie uses to express herself. It's high-pitched, clipped, full of excitement. It's a blend of anticipation and joy and hope. And yet, it somehow shrieks with a tone of frustration, as well. I call it her "passion" bark.

It typically occurs in the dark of night, preceded with the sound of running dog toes, the slap of the doggy door, a quick call over her shoulder to come see ... come see ... come see ...!

I've tried to let her bark it out by herself. But this particular sound will not be ignored nor denied. I am compelled to stumble from a warm bed, locate slippers and flashlight, and go see ... go see ... go see ...!

And, on one such recent middle-of-the-night call, I saw.

I knew there had been a pesky, opinionated, opossum with a well-honed talent for annoying dogs, hanging around the vicinity; more specifically, nesting in the outside rafters of my guest cottage. I had poked and prodded and banged away with broomsticks and branches, hoping to dislodge the unwanted lodger, and convince it to move on. I succeeded in really irritating it and reenforcing its resolve to stay. But then there had been several weeks of silence. Either it had relocated to a quieter neighborhood, or Sophie and the critter had reached a pact of peaceful coexistence, I naively believed.

And then it came. The barking bordering on hysteria. The doggy meltdown. It was 3:00 a.m. I scraped myself off the ceiling and stubbed my bare feet across the backyard rocks to reach Sophie as she was throwing herself bodily against the back fence, trying to climb it. Perched on the top of the six-foot-high wooden barrier was a very large, very surly, smarty-pants opossum hurling spit-filled insults into the face of Sophie's passion and being.

I thought my mere arrival would run the critter off. I tried turning the flashlight full into its eyes. I used the age-old proven verbal threat of the superior being: "Shoo! Shoo!" All of which just made him more determined. Sophie was looking at me with unabashed trust and expectation. I couldn't let her down. I grabbed a stout stick from the ground (possibly the one that had so effectively done the poking weeks earlier). I thrust it in his direction, and he grasped it with a vice-like grip and a look in his eyes that said: "You and what army, little missy ..."

The struggle became a literal seesaw across the fence – me on one side, the devil creature on the other. The more I tilted it, the harder he gripped and the louder he cursed in his growly sort of way. At one point, the pendulum swung at an angle that had him dangling over Sophie's head. "Oh, goody! A piñata," I could almost hear her thoughts. But I couldn't go through with it, so I swung him back to the other side of the fence. I gave the branch a last heave-ho and let it fly. There was a thud. An "oooof." Silence, as Sophie and I waited, listening. Then scampering feet and fading insults.

Sophie and I retired to the kitchen for some well-earned cookies and juice to re-live the experience.

Passion has its side of frustration, doesn't it? I've discovered this more and more of late with my own commitment to authoring and publishing books. It's not like I have a choice really – any more than Sophie does with her blood-deep passion for the hunt. We both have our share of satisfaction and joys, of course. But we both also have our narcissistic meltdowns when things don't simply drop on our side of the fence.

In the end, however, I've found that passions simply won't be denied or ignored. They are what they are. Unique to each and every one of us – as telling as Sophie's special bark, as much a part of us as our very souls. And, I suppose, all one can do is keep on chasing them.

Hopefully, we all also have at least one friend who is willing to get up in the middle of the night with us ... and bring along an encouraging heart, a big stick, and cookies.

(February 3, 2010)

And he's back.

Even Sophie had given up. A very rare occurrence. My mixed-breed dog Sophie can be the most tenacious of creatures, once she sets her mind to a thing. But she's also very smart. And, perhaps, she knew the risks and frustrations would outweigh the benefits at this point.

I'm writing about an opossum that began plaguing us well over three months ago. I even wrote a column about it. A sassy sort of being – all full of vinegar and determination and smart remarks. We had finally experienced a 3:00 a.m. showdown, which ended in our calling it a draw, I guess. He walked away in a huff; Sophie and I went in for cookies. No harm, no foul. And, at last, he seemed to be gone.

As I said, even Sophie had become silent on the subject. No more midnight meltdowns and super-excited barking at the just-out-of-reach cottage rafters where he had staked his claim. Then, a few weeks ago, the human cottage resident began reporting the same old familiar scratchy opossum noises of moving in and settling down taking place.

This time, we called in the pros. Still determined that no one should be harmed, we consulted with an expert from North Augusta. She brought me a special opossum-sized live-trap and even set it up, complete with peanut butter on crackers for an irresistible come-on. After several days, we did catch one extremely irritated squirrel. I noticed when I released him, that, despite the foul language and threats and comments on my character, he had stayed calm enough to devour the peanut-butter-crackers.

We waited and waited and waited. No opossum. No squirrels. No moving day for the critter in question. He was still calmly coming and going, in and out of the rafters apartment – walking right past the entrance to the inviting trap. Opossums can not be that smart, I reasoned. Maybe it was the bait or the position of the trap.

I decided to replace the old stuff (now complete with chocolate chip cookies and a few different kinds of yummies) and reposition the opening to better align with the rafters entrance. Climbing a stepladder with fresh crackers in hand, the ladder went one way and I went in the opposite direction, landing awkwardly on one leg and then my back.

Of course, no other human was around. But Sophie was immediately at my side (she first ran the other way as she saw me coming down ... a smart dog, indeed). She was ever so solicitous, sniffing me and licking my face asking if I was hurt and what could she do to help. I must admit, I thought I had broken my leg and was hesitant to look, convinced I would see bones everywhere. So I lay very still with my eyes shut tight. I appreciated Sophie's soft kisses and concern, and felt comforted and cherished. Then, ever so lightly, I felt her nose examine my hand, and slowly pull the crackers away in her gentle lips. "Do you want me to just hold those for you?" I could almost hear her say. Sweet, caring, Sophie – the truth will out! But it did make me laugh. And what better antidote for severe pain and fear than someone who can make you laugh?

The leg was not broken. In fact, it didn't even have the decency to swell up or turn black-and-blue. It just caused an embarrassing limp for a couple of weeks and difficulty sitting in one place for very long. And, perhaps, it gave me an equally uncomfortable lesson. I wonder if our own expressions of concern for others might sometimes be tinged with self-serving motives. Do our inquiries of "what can I do" ever cover up "what's in it for me"? Or perhaps the cracker was truly an afterthought. And, either way, I was comforted and made to feel better, so perhaps it doesn't really matter, as long as we are simply there to help one another.

In the end, Sophie did get the cracker, but stayed loyally at my side anyway. I learned a couple of good lessons and have now also promised to never climb a ladder again without a proper "spotter."

Alas, the trap remains impotent and empty.

And the opossum roams free.

(May 2, 2010)

TEDDY'S SONG.

"You are my sunshine, my only sunshine.
You make me happy when skies are grey.
You'll never know dear how much I love you.
Please don't take my sunshine away."

It's the only song my father has ever learned to play on the piano; he used it to impress my mother when they were courting (although she, herself, was a music major and continues to be a piano teacher). So the song goes pretty far back in my collection of childhood memories. A source for a good giggle or two, when Dad would play it and tell his courting stories.

"You are my sunshine ..." I don't know why I began to sing it to my mixed-breed dog Teddy. It was shortly after he came to live with us – an escapee from a life of unhappiness, without love and nurturing, devoid of appreciation and laughter; all the things that make life worth living for any of us, the things he deserved and needed to know. It was four years ago (five this coming July). He and my other mixed breed dog, Sophie, hit it off immediately. I joke that Sophie is my dog and Teddy is Sophie's dog. But Teddy and I have a special relationship all our own. A hugs and laughter and dancing type of personal bond with each other.

"My only sunshine ..." It began in the kitchen. I started singing the song rather loudly and rather badly to him. Sophie left the room, but it made Teddy laugh. So I added dance steps and hand motions, and sang all the verses I knew. And he laughed even more – from eyes to tail and on tiptoe. From then on, it became his signature song. To date, he has lived up to every word of it.

"You make me happy when skies are grey ..." Whenever I arrive home from being away, he dances as if he is inviting me to sing it for him. When he does a good thing (like alerting me to someone at the front door), he lights up and knows he has done something

good and pleasing and wants to hear "his song" again. When he is afraid of the thunder, he tucks his head on my lap and asks me to sing away the anxiousness. When I don't feel well or am sad, he cuddles at my side and, I think, wishes he could sing it to me to cheer me up as well.

"I only know dear how much I love you..." Teddy came to me broken and bruised and almost used up at the innocent age of four. Today he is eight – perhaps he will be nine at his next (approximate) birthday in July. Perhaps not. I just learned that Teddy has cancer. Possibly the hard life he had been dealt early predisposed him to it. I don't know. Don't really care. What I do care about is making his last few weeks as love-filled and happy as we have made the last few years for each other.

I believe Sophie knows. Sophie is wise about such things. She plays more gently with him. But she still includes him in her games. And I will continue to sing his song to him, and we will dance on the kitchen floor as long as he is able – right up until that time when God will see fit to take him back to the source of all the sunshine itself.

"Please don't take my sunshine away ..." I am better for having loved Teddy. But he will be achingly missed. And my world has already grown a bit darker for his getting ready to leave it.

(June 6, 2010)

THE LOVE TREE.

Halfway down Magnolia Street, along a quiet stretch of rough red dirt road, now partially hidden behind gangly weeds and scruffy underbrush, there looms a gnarled and ancient reminder of sweet, long-remembered love blooming in Aiken.

On a recent morning walk with Sophie, my best canine pal, we first saw a woman standing on the side of that road, peering with deep interest toward a huge old magnolia tree. As we came nearer, we noticed two young boys scrambling over the lower limbs of the tree, calling out, "I've found one ... here's another one!" Sophie and I stopped to join in.

"It's the love tree," the woman explained. For at least 40 or 50 years, she told me, young people living in the area – her daughters included – climbed this tree, which was now being explored by her grandsons. Remnants of a homemade tree fort still remain about halfway up its sturdy trunk and lie in scraps around its base. In addition to the challenge of the climb and the secrets shared in its hideaway, custom demanded that if you held someone special in your heart, you documented your feelings by carving your and your beloved's initials into the great arms of that tree. Sometimes, the letters were even enclosed within a carefully etched shape of a heart.

Sophie and I cautiously crunched our way through the undergrowth to get a closer look. The woman pointed out the initials she could remember and those the boys had just found. But half a century of growth lifted many of them out of range, or left only mild streaks in its deeply furrowed bark. Years of summer rains covered many branches with a thick coating of moss. Perhaps the wise magnolia was protecting her young lovers from discovery or uninvited curiosity after so many years of secret-keeping. I felt a bit like an eavesdropper on private conversations – regardless of how many years ago they might have been whispered. Still, I ran my finger along the faint, jagged shape of a "W," and around the right-hand curve of a still-visible heart. I squinted against the sky to see what may have been a "J" and still more indiscernible etchings higher up.

We tapped our toes against fallen limbs and lamented the potential loss of this reminder of simpler days and innocence. But then we noticed the new growth sprouting with great promise from some of the tree's lower limbs. Tightly furled leaves and blossoms looked strong and healthy and supple against new green branches. We smiled at each other and talked of the hope this gave us that the tree as well as its memories and customs would continue for yet another century, and perhaps another and another.

And so, Sophie and I continued on our walk and discussed this unexpected find. It made me smile. And yet, somehow I was not terribly surprised to have been introduced to a "love tree" on Magnolia Street. It is, after all, just one more quiet symbol of remembrance and hope and sweetness that surrounds me in this remarkable town. A reminder that gentleness and love have a long and lasting history here, and continue to be alive and well and blooming in the heart of Aiken.

(August 22, 2010)

THE DUCK WITH WHITE FEATHERS.

She's still there – the duck with white feathers that graces the Carolina Bay near my house and haunts my imagination. She's still there, floating with pristine loneliness across the murky surface of the water. Each season, I hold my breath a bit until I spot her – surviving, searching, alive, alone – still there.

It's been several years now. She arrived with a companion, a dark shadow of herself. They swam and chattered and walked together, made a life together. But one day he was gone; while she, for reasons known only to her own heart, decided to stay. Since then, others have come – in flocks or alone. She welcomes them with gratitude and hospitality and cajoles them to remain with her, but none do. The only one that seems to return again and again to offer her some quiet, distant company is the Blue Heron. He swoops and stands aloof, but must be a bit of comfort for her. A familiar being. Another lone presence.

All through the summer heat and droughts that dry her home to hardened, ghost-gray clay; and then through harsh winter cold that coats her world with icy crust; in spite of storms that crash down pines and slick the earth barren or flood it past its capacity, she survives and never seems to falter. Each time I come again to look for her, she's there.

Day after day, she goes about her life. Dipping below the surface of the water, prowling the shores, tending to her feathery beauty. Sometimes she browses for the occasional visitor who may have treats and food to supplement her meager pantry. But she never seems to expect anything. Accepting the fact that you may have come to simply walk the dog and gaze across the water and pass her by. I always mean to bring her a bit, but never seem to remember, and feel the worse for it.

I think what amazes me the most about her is her complete unawareness of the fact that she brings such beauty and grace to the Bay – and to the lives of those who watch her. She doesn't know that I look for her, that I am in awe of her perseverance and courage, that I write about her. She simply pursues her day-by-day, with forthright unselfconsciousness. I even wrote a poem about her once. The only poem I ever tried to write. But she moved that part of my soul where the poetry lives, and so I put it down to remember.

And then I realized that beyond her simple loveliness, I was in deepest admiration of the example she set to those who would truly see her. That her courage despite her life experiences, her lack of self-pity or even self-awareness, her never-failing openness to what would come her way, was exactly what I hoped to find in my own heart, my own life. I suspect it's what most of us search for in the end. I also suspect that to unknowingly, unexpectedly, unaware, touch the lives of those who simply pass us by would, in the end, be a life very well done.

(February 13, 2011)

"Baby" says: com'on in.

Empty red and black leatherette chairs sit waiting, tucked beneath the aprons of Formica and faux-wood metal tables. Old, country radio music comforts the air and almost drowns out the constant hum of the exhaust fan. The floor is tidy, but as worn and dated as the music. The walls are fresh-painted over old wood and dotted with handmade signs printed on thin colored paper about hot dogs and other specialties. Once-proud awards are framed and hung there, too, to remind folks of a long-time history of fame and allure. Overhead, ancient fluorescent tubes glare from the high narrow ceiling. Some are yellow, some white, a few are burned-out and blank as they stare impotently into the room below. Mismatched hanging fans turn and stir the smells of bacon and burgers and an open grill.

The cook – who more than slightly resembles a younger, larger, less effusive, and infinitely tougher Willy Nelson – wears a black kerchief tied tightly around his forehead and long braided hair. He scrapes the grill with a practiced rhythm, turning the beef and toasted buns, shaking the fries from bubbling oil, all in one fluid motion. Then he reaches for the next order fluttering near his head, clothes-pinned to a thin silver wire. Plastic plates and paper cups are stacked against the wall within his long reach.

"Hey, Baby," the waitresses call out to long-time patrons and strangers alike.

"How's your dog doin', Hon?" one asks as she rings up a bill.

Another experienced staff member places an iced tea on the high counter top that stretches down half the length of the room as a new customer approaches and pulls himself into one of the black swivel seats.

"Thanks," he smiles, knowing his "usual" would be there waiting for him.

"Hey, Hon ... coffee's brewin'," the first woman calls to another walk-in. Her words float over on the fragrance of her promise – strong and warm and familiar.

There are even more empty chairs now. A few stragglers worry over the economy and old trucks breaking down and old dogs wearing out. But it is much too quiet, in spite of the ever-present exhaust fan.

Time was, not very long ago – perhaps just a couple of years or so – when it was difficult to find a spot to sit in this one-of-a-kind place. People jostled inside the door and shared tables with strangers or friends they happened to meet there. Burgers and fries and chili and cokes all vied for space on the tables and counter top. It wasn't just a great burger and fries joint (and the best patty melt this side of your cardiac doctor's office) – it was "A Place." It never claimed to be anything more than it was. And it never failed to live up to its reputation. A "guilty pleasure." A step back in time. A real place, with real people. A place where everybody is called "Baby" and "Hon" regardless of age or length of acquaintance. A place that serves a real sit-down-waitress-delivered breakfast – with a "last call" when the eggs run out and the grill gets primed for lunch and dinner. A place that used to take cash only when you brought your check up to the counter (but has now succumbed to the modern need to credit-card everything).

But where have all the people gone?

I worry about this, because I suspect we need these places as much as we need our memories. And I am quite convinced there is infinite value in the comfort food they supply ... as well as being called "Baby" on a really bad day, and having your favorite beverage waiting for you on the counter because you're just that special.

In the end, I would like to think that we could all benefit in some small way by dropping back in to Arri's Grill again – right where it's always been, along the back side of Mitchell Shopping Center, just off of Whiskey Road.

Tell 'em "Baby" told you it was time to get on back home again.

(March 13, 2011)

ARRI'S
GRILL
OPEN

Finding emeralds in the forest.

Suddenly, I was afraid. The trees were bending in, whispering things I couldn't understand. The breeze still carried a wintry chill. My footsteps crunched on broken leaves and pine straw, echoing through the brush like phantom footfalls starting and stopping just behind me (but cleverly hiding whenever I turned to look). Sophie, my canine companion, had run too far ahead.

It was early spring. The first bright sun in days had warmed the sky into a fantastically deep, smooth blue, clean and cloudless. I had invited Sophie to join me for a walk in one of our once-in-a-while places – the State Nature Area, a bit of a drive from our home, but a new adventure every time we go there. This was an unexplored path for us, not well traveled and tramped down, perhaps not even a path. I was beginning to feel the fear. It crept up with that unmistakable chill sliding around my heart and inching its way up my spine. "Sophie, wait for me!" I tried to call out in a voice that only her ears could hear, without alerting the ghosts and snakes and ne'er-do-wells that were now creeping and hiding and closing in all around me. She looked over her shoulder at me, but apparently could not see the imminent danger, so slowed up only a bit.

We came to a fallen tree. It stuck up high into the air with dead and dying branches and was far too long to circumvent around either end. Perhaps this would be a good place to turn and retreat, I remember thinking. But Sophie scrambled under it with ease and turned instead to beg me to follow. Hesitatingly, I found enough space to climb over it. Its barky fingers and dried broken limbs caught at my coat, trying to hold me back. I shivered loose and forged ahead, pleading with Sophie to "wait for me ... wait for me!"

The path was getting weaker now. But just ahead, through a tangle of barren tree branches and long, waving grasses, I could catch a glimpse of water. A tributary filled with recent rains now sparkled in the sunlight. So inviting, mesmerizing, enchanting, it drew me forward, away from my fear. I stepped out of the shadows, and could see it clearly now. A bed of emeralds! Just under the surface of the water, glittering in the reflection of the sun, bright, green, shining with intrigue and beauty, was a bed of glorious, polished emeralds.

As I crept closer, I could make out their form. They were, in fact, emerald-colored plants, tiny and perfectly shaped, one like the next and the next. They looked like miniature palm trees, anchored into the mud below, with their delicate fronds just breaking the surface of the water, half floating at the edge between wetlands and air. The sun, at just the right angle, was pulling at them, reflecting off of their wondrous beauty, turning them into sparkling gems.

I needed to touch them. Leaning in close, Sophie now curious and at my side, I stroked their loveliness. They were soft and giving, and not a bit off-putting with a residue I half expected from a still-life pond. I wanted to pick one, but stopped to consider my right to do so – to interrupt the magic. Sophie sniffed at them, put her paw against them. They rippled and laughed and waved in response.

Now, it was time to leave. Not in retreat out of fear, but in awe of the beauty we had found on the other side of it.

I wonder how many of us live afraid. With ghosts and unseen shadows haunting our minds and footsteps, creeping ever closer behind us. I suspect that, too often, we get caught up in the rough, cragginess of life, unable to see beyond the broken branches, focusing on the brokenness alone. I suspect we feel abandoned at times – calling out "wait for me ... wait for me." Perhaps we should simply try to look for what may be right in front of us, sparkling in the sun, just waiting to be discovered, just on the other side of the fallen debris ... the emeralds in the forest, on the other side of fear. *(April 3, 2011)*

Speaking in Drums.

My feet were cold and wet. My back was starting to ache. My mind was wandering. And then he entered the tent. He brought drums. Quite a few drums. Some tall, some squat, all beautifully shaped. And he handed out tambourines. And put things around on tabletops that looked like small, flat picture frames – round, square, rectangle. In place of pictures, however, these funny little frames held a sort of odd, smooth material. The frame items were just placed there, on several of the tables, in front of no one in particular, but available to anyone who wanted to touch and hold and experience them. I learned later these frames without pictures are called "sound shapes." How delightfully descriptive, I thought: sound shapes. I played one. Or perhaps I spoke with one. Or expressed my emotions – or heard my emotions – or actually created my own emotions – through one. It was an amazing experience.

The tent where this experience took place was on the grounds of Aiken Prep School. It was during the recent "Prep Fest" event held to benefit a number of highly worthy, not-for-profit organizations, as well as the school itself. It was raining and colder than it should have been. But there were plenty of tents and wonderful music and delicious food and people across the generations having a great deal of fun.

I was signing books, and was somewhat confined to my space. So when the man with the drums entered the tent where I was, and began smiling and drumming and pulling us into his world, it was most welcome. He didn't say much, if anything, with his human voice (I truthfully don't remember). But he was eloquent with his hands, his beat, his <u>drum</u> voice. Without being verbally invited, we began to join in. Some of us on the other drums, some with tambourines, some with the "sound shapes," some with nothing more than our hands and hearts.

The drum voices sang and sang and sang. He changed the rhythm on us a few times. And he stopped and talked to us about rhythm and cadence a bit. He compared words to drum beats, and verbal communication to this more primal form of speaking.

I sat with him later and found out his name is Northal Gaddy. He goes by the short name of "Not," which I thought was the absolute opposite of what it should be for such an exceptionally positive man. He practices this art of what is called "Health Rhythms" under the descriptive business name of "I Drum To You - Recreational Health Drum Circles" (idrum2U). He explained the philosophical meaning of drumming "to you" as giving something to someone without expecting anything in return. What I experienced, however, was that he gave each of us within hearing distance an "invitation" to join in. Like a thrown ball that no one can refuse to throw back. He told me about his experiences working with the disadvantaged and disconnected, adults as well as kids, corporations as well as individuals. He talked about the healing aspects of his calling, the universality of it, its ancient roots. And he smiled deeply as he remembered playing with the master drummers of Ghana.

Later, I researched more into this philosophy and practice and learned about how these healing drums can help one's capacity to cope with stress, how they provide mind-nurturing exercise to modify thinking, how they can raise the mind above our troubles, disorders, and self-doubt. It's called by the experts "intrepidness," or "resolute fearlessness." Personally, I'd call it simply wicked great fun!

Too soon, we had to stop in deference to the other musical presentations. But the experience continues to be with me somehow. Just as Mr. Gaddy's business name also keeps dancing around in my head with a highly personal message and significance. "I drum to you." A gift, thrown with love, blindly and hopefully out into the world, for someone – anyone – whoever is out there – to perhaps pick it up and throw it right back.

And with that final thought ... *"I write to you."*

(March 11, 2012)

About This Book

The first column I ever wrote for the *Aiken Standard* is not included in this book. I looked back at it, reread it, and I realized I was simply trying to introduce myself to this town that had so recently become my home. I wanted to let Aiken know that I was quite captivated at first sight; and now, I was becoming even more charmed by it, falling in love with it more deeply with each passing day. And, like any new relationship, it was a hesitant attempt at first. A hopeful plea that the other would like me right back.

As I grew into Aiken, I grew into my own voice for the columns. I wrote from my heart. I wrote exactly what I saw, what I felt, what I experienced. And Aiken continued to welcome me with open arms and invitations.

By the eighth column, I had finally discovered what I had been searching for. What I wanted to do was to try and capture the strong "sense of place" I was feeling in this amazing town with its gracious people and unique opportunities. That eighth column was titled "The Rhythm of Aiken." It's the first column I chose to include in this book.

Not surprisingly, a couple of years later, when I began to write my first novel – based very much on my experiences in Aiken as documented by my columns – the title for the novel became "The Rhythm of Selby" (the town of Selby being a thinly veiled Aiken). Of course, I mixed in plenty of fiction, but it was great fun to share my experiences – all gathered together – with folks right here as well as far away.

More recently, and more than a hundred columns later, I found myself being strongly urged by my readers to compile the actual columns themselves into book format.

It was wonderfully nostalgic going back through the files and clippings and reading about what I was feeling at the time, the new experiences I was realizing, the new friends I was making.

Due to the sheer number of them, however, my publisher convinced me to bring them out in two volumes; this, obviously, is the first.

Although I believe strongly in the "theater of the mind" – creating word pictures so vivid that a reader can envision for himself a place or time or scene – I also decided to include some actual photographs in this book. Perhaps this was in deference to the "Barbaras" out there that would not want to believe without seeing. More likely, however, it is because Aiken is so terribly visual. With every curve in a dirt road, just beyond every forest tree, in the glow of every sunrise, and the halo of the Carolina moon, rests a new and visually captivating scene. At least it does for me.

So, most of this photography was taken by me, an admitted amateur, but seen through my eye and my camera lens. A few photos were generously shared with me by friends (acknowledged on page 2). But, for the most part, this is the way I see my Aiken. Both verbally and visually. I hope it is (or will be) yours, as well.

Thank you for believing.

OTHER BOOKS BY MARTI HEALY

Marti Healy is fond of saying that she tries to never write the same book twice. Consequently, her published works are varied in theme and structure, but consistent with their upbeat, "G-rated" subject matter. Each strikes a chord with her audience that makes every reader feel like a special friend of the author, a favorite companion for sharing a cup of tea and a good story.

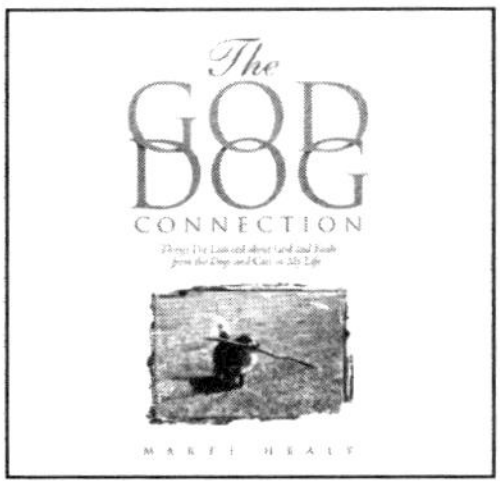

Marti's first published book, **THE GOD-DOG CONNECTION**, is subtitled: *"Things I've Learned about God and Faith from the Dogs and Cats in My Life."* It is a collection of 25 essays that each captures a vignette of animal behavior, and then the faith lesson that can be drawn from it. Now in its second printing, this delightful, gentle and warm work has been enthusiastically embraced by mainstream readers literally around the world. The book recently received a warm endorsement by well-known actress and animal advocate, **BETTY WHITE**, who said of it: ***"It is always a joy to find a fellow animal lover who not only reads the animals accurately - but listens to them! A lovely book."***